PRAISE FOR THE FAMILY QUARTERBACK

"Travis Turner joined the University of Nebraska football team as a walk-on player in the early 1980's. As his coach I observed his journey from walk-on to starting quarterback and the struggles he encountered along the way which he chronicles. More importantly, he relates the struggles he encountered in his spiritual journey as a player, husband and father. Travis has gained a level of maturity and insight which makes this book not only very interesting from an athletic perspective, but of vital importance to anyone who seeks to have a meaningful relationship with Christ and seeks to integrate his or her faith into interpersonal relationships involving family, friends and associates."

—TOM OSBORNE
Former Head Coach, University of Nebraska

"Without the wisdom, counsel and spiritually mature guidance of Travis Turner, I would not have the marriage and family I have today. Through my years as a pro-family ministry leader, political candidate, and now leading a Christian university, Travis Turner constantly challenged me to be a better husband, and a better father to our 8 now grown children. I am so excited that, through publication of "The Family Quarterback," untold thousands will have the same opportunity to be blessed and challenged by Travis to be the husbands and fathers God created them to be!"

—LEN MUNSIL, B.S., J.D.
President, Arizona Christian University

"I have known and loved Travis and Carol Turner for over twenty five years. They love the Lord, they love each other, and they are dedicated to helping others make their marriages a blessing. In The Family Quarterback, Travis leaves it all on the field. He is not pretending he has always been a great husband. He shares honestly and openly about his mistakes and the lessons he has learned that have enabled him to triumph over sin, the flesh and the devil, so that he can be the man God created him to be. Travis is the godly quarterback of his family and he lives a life that is a great example for every husband. Those who take in the wisdom of this book and apply it will discover the blessings that God intends for all of our marriages."

—MARK BUCKLEY
Senior Pastor, Living Streams Church, Phoenix, Arizona

THE FAMILY QUARTERBACK

Every Man's Playbook for Effective Leadership

FOOTBALL PRINCIPLES THAT WORK IN THE GAME OF LIFE

TRAVIS TURNER

THE FAMILY QUARTERBACK
Every Man's Playbook for Effective Leadership

DIVINE ROMANCE
MINISTRIES

5121 E. Charter Oak
Scottsdale, AZ 85254
www.DivineRomanceMinistries.org

ISBN 978-0-9907629-0-4

Printed in the United States of America by Epic Print Solutions

Cover design by Rodjie Ulanday

DEDICATION

This book is dedicated to my best friend, Carol Wilson Turner. Without your patience, kindness and keen eye, this project would not have happened. Your selfless love has transformed me. I will forever be grateful for your willingness to love me unconditionally. The best part of me, has always been you!

CONTENTS

PREFACE

For twenty-some years, I have talked about writing a book. I started at least a half dozen outlines that I had hoped would materialize into a manuscript, but it never did. In reality, I lacked the confidence and the patience. I also let the distractions of life get in the way. After I turned fifty, I realized in the summer of 2013, I needed to start writing or it would never happen.

As I watched *College Game Day* on ESPN one Saturday morning, I realized the book needed to be structured around football. Our culture thrives on football. We can't get enough of it. So, with that in mind, I began contemplating this story line in the hopes that the message I have to tell will be of interest to men who need to hear what I have to say. Like a winning football coach, I've got a game plan for them. What I am hoping is that a man who wouldn't normally read a book about how to be a Godly husband and father, might be willing to read a book about how to be a successful quarterback.

In this book the football analogies I use will tell stories about family life and will give instructions on how to be a successful husband, in a camouflaged way. You see, these concepts I'm sharing from my own life experiences combined with the truth of the Bible, are the real heart of this book. I have integrated various lifestyle habits for men that can change their lives and have a dramatic impact on their relationships.

What I most want readers to know is that they can walk moment by moment with the creator of the universe. It is about developing an intimate relationship with Jesus Christ. I believe that any man who has accepted Jesus Christ into his life has the ability to understand and lead his family effectively. The question is, will this man, whom I will be calling to lead his family effectively, be willing to surrender his life, and to learn what it takes to make a marriage last a lifetime? That is the only way we can transform our selfish, sinful, wretched selves into stories of redemption—the ultimate way to win the game of life.

In the following section I call Pre-game Warm Up I outline my own story of God's redemption in my marriage and in my life.

Since football will be our template, I have divided each subsequent chapter into four quarters:

- **First Quarter - A story centered on football that helps illustrate the central principle of the chapter.**
- **Second Quarter: The Play - The primary focus of the chapter is a habit or priority that the family quarterback needs to incorporate into his daily life.**
- **Third Quarter: Reading the Defense -** The first thing the quarterback looks for when he comes to the line of scrimmage is the threats the opposing defensive unit presents. These threats are our opponent's schemes to derail "the play." A successful quarterback never underestimates his adversary.
- **Fourth Quarter: The Red Zone - This is the most significant place on the field. In life, it is our home. In this context, I will share stories from my family experience that will illustrate application of "the play."**

Use of Scripture

Most of the biblical references used in this book will be from the New International Version, unless otherwise indicated. I am not a theologian, a Bible scholar, or even a seminary graduate. I am, however, an avid student of the Word because the Bible has literally changed my life. At times, I will take some liberty with my use of scripture. I hope it doesn't offend your sensibilities. My goal is to inspire every husband and father to be the man God created him to be.

It's time to look in the mirror. We are the quarterbacks of our families. We are the leaders, and everyone is looking to us for guidance and direction. To our families we are like Peyton Manning, Drew Brees, or Russell Wilson. Our families are depending on us to lead them to the Promised Land.

PRE-GAME WARM UP: REDEMPTION

Every football game starts with the entire team lining up for stretching exercises. We will begin this book in a similar way. The following chapters contain numerous Nebraska football stories, interspersed with family tales from our twenty-nine years of marriage. To put these anecdotes in context, you need a proper warm up. To do that, I'll share my account of God's redemption of me and our family. It is the foundation for our entire existence.

I met Carol Lynn Wilson in the summer of 1984. I believe that was divine intervention. There is no other way to explain it.

I had just finished my sophomore year at the University of Nebraska in Lincoln (UNL). Carol had recently transferred to UNL from Nebraska Wesleyan University. As she prepared for this change, Carol specifically prayed that she would not be distracted by anything, *especially a man*, during this season of her life.

I was resurrecting my football career. After struggling for three years, I had earned a scholarship and was contending for the starting quarterback position. I had recommitted my life to Jesus for the umpteenth time, and I was trying to live according to the Gospel. The area of my life that was still very much undisciplined was my moral convictions. I had lost my virginity in high school. Girls were a real problem for me. I was a womanizer. I knew this had to change.

Unlike me, Carol had rarely dated. She had protected herself from men like me. She was not interested in building a new relationship, especially with someone like me.

In July that summer, I attended a Fellowship of Christian Athletes (FCA) gathering at Johnson Lake in central Nebraska. I participated because of what I thought to be the Lord's direction. I had no idea who was going to attend. At the Lord's prompting, I was continually being encouraged to go, so much so that He even "told" me who to call for a ride. I could not shake off these promptings, so I reluctantly gave teammate Brad Johnson a call to see if he could take me.

While in name I called myself a Christian at that time, I felt I still didn't fit in with the other Christians at the camp. I was trying to live for Christ, but I had not made any Christian friends. I barely knew Brad, so it was an awkward trip as we drove to the lake. I was an outsider to this group. I didn't even know who to talk to. While I was there, I felt like everyone was trying to change me and turn me into a Christian.

As we arrived, it was dinner time. A beautiful blonde young lady invited me inside the dining hall to eat. That was the first time I saw Carol. She radiated a warmth, a kindness, and a compassion that I couldn't resist. I was smitten. Okay, I was obsessed. I didn't let her out of my sight the entire weekend.

In a flash, the weekend was over. As a way of continuing my pursuit of Carol, I talked her into letting me ride with her and her friend to western Nebraska. Her friends tried to warn her about me. They didn't appreciate the attention I was giving her. They called me "Travis the Tiger" or "Trav the Mav."

When we finally returned to Lincoln, she tried to give me the brush off. I wasn't having it. I kept asking her out, and she would reluctantly agree. She wanted us to "just be friends." Of course, that was never my intention.

As time passed, Carol decided to try to blow my mind by inviting me to her home church. It was an Assemblies of God congregation. She thought the loud music, raising hands, and praying aloud would get rid of me. She didn't realize that in the past I had attended a Pentecostal church with my brother and I loved it. In a final effort to elude me, she invited me to dinner with her pastor and his wife. She suspected they would tell her I was bad news. She didn't expect them to really like me. Surprisingly Pastor Dave Argue accepted me. He offered to become my first mentor. We met weekly for study, prayer, and counsel.

That October, I bought an engagement ring. I planned to ask Carol to marry me after the football season. I was now the starting quarterback and, as a result, I had many invitations to share my Christian testimony. I was an instant celebrity and I took advantage of every opportunity I was given. She traveled with me to churches, banquets, and events all over the state.

The night I had planned to propose, I ended up in the hospital with staph infection. I told Carol about my plan, and she said "not now." This did not faze me. Undaunted, in the next two months, I asked her two more times with same result.

Our relationship stayed somewhat the same until that following January. While I went to the Sugar Bowl in New Orleans, Carol attended a missions conference in Urbana, Illinois. When we both returned to Lincoln, she finally gave in to my persistence and accepted the ring.

Not long after, we went through the typical pre-marital counseling. It was a six-week commitment with different elders and pastors of our church. In one meeting, we took the Taylor-Johnson temperament evaluation. Pastor Dave laughed when he read us the results. We were off-the-page opposites. He told us, "There will never be a dull moment with you two." Boy was he prophetic.

During our engagement, my struggles with sexual desire continued to haunt me. I wanted to be involved with Carol sexually as a part of our relationship. I pushed her until she finally gave in. She was a virgin and I did not respect her desire to wait until after our wedding ceremony. My indiscretion in not honoring her wishes cost us a great deal of insecurity, pain, and distrust. It would take ten years of marriage to resolve it completely. My greatest regret of our engagement, and perhaps my life, was not protecting Carol from *ME*, sexually.

A short time before Carol and I were to be married, one of my teammates asked, "Why do you want to get married?" Without thinking, I quickly responded, "It's better to marry, than to burn with lust." I was quoting 1 Corinthians 7:9. What I didn't realize was that my spontaneous response revealed my true inner motivation.

This hidden agenda would become evident early in our marriage. It would prove to be a major obstacle for us to overcome. Because of my faulty thinking and my questionable morals, I believed that marriage would solve my lust problem. Unfortunately, to my dismay, not only did marriage not relieve my morals problem, it revealed it.

We were a classic clash of lifestyles. I was unprepared for that. Carol was a carpenter's daughter. Her father built their home with his bare hands. More than that, her mother died when Carol was sixteen. The grief of the loss of her mother would, in many ways, define her. It turned out that Carol had to care for a father who didn't have time or patience for her. To make matters worse, her older brother abused her at a young age.

In order to make a life for herself, Carol rode her bike everywhere instead of relying upon others for transportation. She worked hard to earn every penny that she had. Likewise, she worked hard to get good grades and to earn an academic scholarship. While she attended college, Carol worked three jobs just to make ends meet.

On the other hand, I was the youngest of five kids. So, as you might imagine, I was spoiled to the core. My father was a car dealer and through the course of my early driving years, I wrecked a lot of them. Because of the family's prosperity, we had motorcycles and boats, along with other things that money could afford. We even lived on "snob hill."

During my youth, my mom took me on shopping sprees. If I broke something, I just bought a new one. Because of this treatment and my success in high school sports, I turned into an entitled athlete who expected others to cater to me.

As our marriage began to take shape, our differences continued to grow. I loved attention and Carol hated it. I was spontaneous, she was calculated. I spent money, she saved it. I like Macy's, she prefers Savers. I enjoy behaving in a fast and furious way, Carol thrives on calm and peace. We are total opposites, so you might think it would make for a perfect fit. Just the opposite was true. I didn't realize how much work it would take for us to fit together as one.

Our wedding day was August 3, 1985. Hundreds of friends and family attended our blessed event. We released red balloons when we left the sanctuary, just like fans at a Husker game after the first score. I had no idea what had just happened. I was just hoping to have sex every day. I figured everything else would take care of itself. What a rude awakening was in store for me.

The honeymoon was painful for Carol. I had sustained some injuries that were taking their toll on my body. I was recovering from knee surgery and had a herniated disc in my back. As a result, we were both disappointed and frustrated by the time we got home. Remember, we were still in college when we started this new life together!

Fall practice started as soon as we got back. Our opening game was against Florida State on national television. Our new life was already rocky, and things were just getting started. Almost every day when I arrived home, Carol was in tears. I didn't know what was going on. I had no capacity to care for her. I was in my own world of hurt, so I had nothing left for her.

We started living in private pain, a place that no one else could see. To make matters worse, we were now a poster couple for Christianity in Nebraska. Because we were prominent in the world of Nebraska Football, we were getting more speaking engagements than ever. Despite our secret pain, we slapped on smiles and we shared our faith, even as our lives were unraveling. Carol's tears continued.

After a traumatic senior season in just about every way, we were rewarded with a trip to Phoenix, Arizona for the Fiesta Bowl. I had a total knee reconstruction after the final regular season game, so I was on crutches when we went to Arizona. While we were there, I spoke at a local church and at the Fellowship of Christian Athletes Fiesta Bowl breakfast. All the while, we kept up our up our "happy couple" front.

During that trip we met several people involved in ministry who would change our lives. One evening we had dinner with Omaha sports anchor John Knicely and his wife, Sue. In the car following that dinner Carol became sick from the smell of the leftover food we had with us. Sue said to her, "I think you are pregnant." Sue was absolutely right!

A test the next day confirmed that our first child was on the way. Wouldn't you know it? More tears from Carol.

We decided to finish school and I stayed with the Husker Football program as a graduate assistant coach. The next spring I was invited back to Phoenix for a conference with professional and college athletes. A year later, that organization invited us to move to Phoenix.

Because of all this attention, it became clear to me that I was a first-round draft pick for God! I wanted to do a work for God and now I could do it. There was a lot I needed to learn when we moved to Arizona. We arrived there on July 10, 1987, and the temperature was 110 degrees! We weren't ready for the heat. Something else I didn't know was that motorcycle riders in Arizona are required to wear eye protection. It didn't take long for me to get pulled over. I thought to myself, "This is your 'welcome to the big city' moment!"

So, there we were in full-time ministry at a mega church in Arizona. Still, the girls kept crying and still, I had no remedy. We started attending a weekly marriage accountability group. This only heated things up. The group focused on my family leadership and my willingness to be like Christ. I was in ministry! Wasn't that being Christ-like enough?

Every week I was confronted with my failure. It was painful. I was doing everything I knew to do. I even changed diapers. Carol and the baby kept crying.

I would travel for speaking events where I sat on stage at a church and prayed for people. I was a rock star in ministry! Everyone loved me. I read my Bible daily. I prayed aloud! I even attended three church services every week. I was trying to save the world. What more could I do? Just the same, Carol and the baby kept crying.

Now, I was starting to get sick of the crying. I was frustrated, angry, and resentful. Nothing I was doing helped.

In our marriage group, we studied the fruit of the Spirit: Love, joy, peace, patience, kindness, goodness, and self-control. I was thinking "I can do that!" The harder I tried, the angrier I got. What I wanted was for Carol to quit crying and give me more sex! It wasn't working. Oh, by the way, she became pregnant again with our second child. More tears!

Two years after being "God's first-round draft pick," and after moving to "paradise" with a mission from the Most High, Carol left me. I was out of control. My resentment owned me. I was so angry I couldn't see straight.

I was broken. My whole life was defined by my own effort. Now those efforts had led to failure. I could not fix this with my own energy, with my own good intensions, or with my own power. Ultimately, I realized that this is what the Spirit of God needed so that He could finally work with me.

I learned I had no solutions for our relationship problems because I was trying to find answers for the wrong questions. I wanted Carol to change, and to give me what I wanted. I wanted her to stop being so emotional. What I didn't recognize was that this was not the problem. I was. I needed to find out why I was so angry. I needed to discover the depth of my immoral perspectives. I needed to rediscover Jesus.

Carol returned home on the condition that I would leave instead. I obliged and I spent a couple of weeks in a friend's spare bedroom to give Carol the needed space. During that time, I left the church and the ministry that brought us to Phoenix. I realized it was time to start over.

I stayed committed to our marriage group. I focused on my attitudes and I began repenting. I began to realize that I had created so much damage I wasn't sure that we could overcome it. It was painful to go back and learn from all my mistakes. I grew weary and it taught me to lean on Christ for my strength. I had always wanted to do a work FOR God, and He just wanted to do a work IN me. I had to totally re-evaluate my Christianity. How could I be full of the Holy Spirit and act like such a jerk to my wife?

With a new kind of thinking, I started to view Carol as an ally instead of an adversary. I began to read the Bible with urgency and reverence. I focused on resolving my resentments and bitterness. I discovered a loving God who would answer my frustration with straightforward kindness. I began to realize how the Lord would speak to me if I gave him time and attention.

God didn't require me to be perfect. He just wanted me to be teachable. He didn't want me to be a rock star. He wanted me to be a rock. He wanted to fill me with His grace, mercy and kindness. He didn't want me to save the world. He wanted me to love my family.

Over the next three years we focused on resolving our conflicts and building harmony. Our marriage group was a source of stability and accountability. Every week we grew in patience and grace with one another. We discovered a depth of love for each other that we didn't even know existed.

Eventually we were asked to share our testimony at seminars around the country. We discovered a passion for helping hurting couples. We found that our struggle was very common in the Christian community. We could see that thousands of marriages were suffering from the same disconnections that we had.

For the past twenty years, Carol and I have been sharing the glorious redemption that we experienced. It has been our privilege to help countless others find this precious gift. The redemption that we experienced is available to anyone. It is our joy to share this story and we pray that God will use it to encourage and strengthen all who hear it.

CHAPTER 1
BUCKLE UP

My freshman year at the University of Nebraska was an incredible, almost unbelievable adventure. I was not attending the school on a football athletic scholarship, but was attempting to make the team as a walk on. I'll never forget the first day I found my locker. It was full of equipment: helmet, shoulder pads, pants, socks, jocks, and cool shoes. I liked that.

One of the first things I noticed was how you couldn't tell the difference between the walk ons and the scholarship guys by assessing the gear we were given, or the lockers we were assigned. Actually, I wasn't even certain who the scholarship players were. The walk ons, like me, outnumbered the other guys three to one. We had more than 100 players on the freshman team, but only twenty-five or so were on full-ride scholarships.

When I put that helmet on for the first time, I felt like a million dollars. Even though the room was filled with great athletes, I felt special just to be there. I felt pretty certain I was a lot faster with those red-swooshed Nike shoes than without them. I still regret that I didn't keep those shoes.

The equipment managers gave us a mesh bag to place sweaty clothes in every day. Imagine that! Someone else did our laundry! I could go to the equipment counter and ask for all kinds of stuff: wristbands, face masks, sweat towels, and special pads. We were catered to like royalty. Some of the best people I ever met were the equipment managers. They had a thankless servant's job. I discovered that if you were nice to them, they were a lot more willing to change out your shoes! After starting out on the freshman squad, fourth team, I worked my way up to sharing first-team duties with a redshirt freshman. I had an above average freshman campaign and after the season was over, I was moved up to varsity scout team duties. That was a big deal for me.

The scout team, or "meat squad" as we were called, had the unique responsibility of running the *opposition's* offense against the Blackshirts—Nebraska's vaunted first team defensive squad. It was a dream come true. I was playing quarterback against one of the top-ranked teams in the country, every single day! I loved every minute of it. It was a thrilling experience to play against the same athletes I had watched on television. I was also a little intimidated.

Late in the season, we were preparing to play a Big Eight opponent and I was running their option offense against our Blackshirt defense. This was a Thursday practice, which usually meant that it was a light practice with no contact. On those days, we wore only shoulder pads, helmets and shorts. It was considered the last major run-through before game day. It was not designed to be very physical, but the intensity was high. It was during these practices that the coaches made certain we were not making mental mistakes. We would practice the same plays repeatedly to eliminate errors.

Because I was an eager underclassman, I had a tendency to run hard on every play. Sometimes the defense didn't like it when I was putting out more effort than they thought necessary. On one particular play, I ran a quarterback option around the right end, perhaps a little more aggressively than I needed to. We'd already run the same play several times.

As I turned the corner to run up field, the strong safety came up and hit me... hard. Really hard! It felt like a Mack Truck had just laid me out. I went flying. My helmet rolled into the end zone and I fell to a heap on the ground. I could hear snickers and hand slaps from the defenders. They were testing me to see how I would handle it. As it turned it certainly wouldn't be the last time I was flattened.

I gathered my senses and got up. I wobbled over to get my helmet that ended up about twenty-five yards away from the play. One of the defensive coaches started walking in my direction. I was expecting him to check on my wellbeing, offer a little sympathy, or better yet, correct the defender who just blew me up. Instead, he said, "You really should buckle your chin strap." This was my "welcome to the varsity football team" moment and I will never forget it. If you are going to play a contact sport, you had better be prepared!

Life is a lot like that. It's not for the faint of heart. You had better be well equipped, and you had better buckle your chinstrap!

The Play: Prepare to be Impacted
"Brace yourself like a man" Job 38:3

The best way to approach this book is to buckle up! Together, we will examine spiritual leadership in the home. YOU and ME. We will carefully examine the scriptural expectations of husbands and fathers. We will evaluate the day-to-day application of His Word in our routines and lifestyle. Since we will be using football to illustrate our principles, this will be a full-contact experience. We will look at the solution to all of our relationship conflicts: CHRIST IN YOU!

Before we get in the game, we must have the proper gear. *"Therefore put on the full armor of God, so that when the day of evil comes, you may be able to stand your ground."* Ephesians 6:13a

Are you ready to stand your ground? If we aren't properly equipped, we are going to get our helmets knocked into the end zone just like I did.

Your Equipment

- **The Belt of Truth Ephesians 6:14a**

   At first glance, this belt appears to be something that keeps your pants up. If you look closer at the text, you will discover that this refers to an entirely different apparatus. A better interpretation comes from the King James Version which says, *"Gird your loins with truth."* I take this to mean protect your manhood with truth. It's a girdle, not a belt.

   The groin is a very sensitive area for the average guy. Getting hit there can ruin you day, or worse.

   The enemy wants to reduce your masculinity. The greatest truth that we need to gird ourselves with is this: *"God created man in His own image."* Genesis 1:27. We are made in His likeness. We are His reflection to the world. What an amazing task and responsibility for us. This truth can become our identity, if we will let it.

   What is your belt of truth? What do you believe? What do you stand for? Since it seems to me that truth in our culture today is relative, absolute thinking does not get much traction. The apostle

Paul gave us an example of a truth that we all could use as a belt to wrap around our waists.

"We are God's workmanship created in Christ Jesus to do good works which God prepared in advance for us to do" Ephesians 2:10

What you believe will dictate how you respond to life. That will ultimately define you.

- **The Breastplate of Righteousness Ephesians 6:14b**

  Have you ever been hit square in the chest? I can tell you that without the protective pads that football players wear, a blow like that will knock you out. Even with pads, players can still have the wind knocked out of them. Quarterbacks are often outfitted with a flak jacket to protector their ribs. More importantly, all of this equipment is used to protect the most important part of the body: the heart. If the heart is damaged, a player becomes incapacitated and ineffective. He may even die.

  One thing that protects our heart from being damaged is righteousness. We are to be *"filled with the fruit of righteousness that comes through Jesus Christ,"* Philippians 3:11a. Christ is the protector of our vital organs. *"And the peace of God, which transcends all understanding, will guard your hearts and your minds in Christ Jesus."* Philippians 4:7.

  On the other hand, if my heart is being protected by my own righteousness, I may have a rough go of it. Scripture asserts, *"There is no one righteous, not even one,"* Romans 3:11a. If we rely on our own goodness, it will result in disabling discouragement, and some blows that could knock us down and out.

- **Feet Fitted with Readiness Ephesians 6:15**

  Proper footwear is an essential part of the football wardrobe. Football shoes come in various styles and materials that combine to provide superior traction on all types of surfaces. Shoes are even designed for specific weather conditions. In every case, football players must wear the appropriate cleats for the field conditions. Wet weather cleats help players move about on a slick surface.

With the right shoe for the job, players don't slip when changing direction and can be extremely effective when they run.

Ephesians talks about our feet being fitted with the readiness of the Gospel of peace. Understanding and depending on peace give us a firm footing. The only place to get authentic peace is from the King of Kings and the Lord of Lords. *"For he (Christ) himself is our peace."* Ephesians 2:14a. Like proper footwear, His peace creates stability and balance so we can navigate the hazardous trials of life.

Similarly, if our steadiness depends on our own understanding, we will only be as stable as our circumstances. We become like Peter when he jumped out of the boat. *"But, when he saw the wind, he was afraid."* Matthew 14:30

- **The Shield of Faith Ephesians 6:16**
  A football player's shoulder pads are his shield. They are an essential piece of protection made with a lightweight, plastic outer shell and lined with high-impact, shock-absorbing foam. Each player has unique shoulder pads suited to his particular position. Linemen have larger, bulkier pads, while quarterbacks and receivers have smaller, lighter pads that do not restrict arm movements.

A man of God has "shoulder pads" of faith to protect him from the lies and schemes of the devil. That faith demonstrates a man's genuine reliance on his heavenly father. Faith is how much we really trust the God we do not see. *"Now faith is confidence in what we hope for and assurance about what we do not see."* Hebrews 11:1

Now for me, my faith has a tendency to be as large as my bank account. If there is plenty of money in the account, I have plenty of faith and I am strong. If the money is running low, or the bills are mounting, my strength is diminished. In like fashion, my ability to fight off the enemy's hostile pursuit dwindles if my faith is weak. I start to look like the man who built his house on sand. *"The rain came down, the streams rose, and the winds blew and beat against that house, and it fell with a great crash."* Matthew 7:27

- **The Helmet of Salvation Ephesians 6:17a**

    Can you imagine a football game without the players wearing helmets? I'm pretty sure it would be a bloody mess. In the early days of football, players did not wear helmets. Over time, helmets have evolved to become highly sophisticated pieces of protective equipment with specialized facemasks. There are at least fifteen facemask styles. The helmet and mask combine to make a vital piece of life-preserving equipment.

    For believers, salvation crowns the head like a helmet. The hope of our salvation provides a helmet for our minds and thoughts. We must prepare for clear thinking. *"I will put my laws in their minds,' declares the Lord."* Hebrews 8:10a. He also assures us *"the mind controlled by the Spirit is life and peace."* Romans 8:6a

    The helmet of salvation helps us to keep our minds on our Redeemer and His kindness. Otherwise, we face trouble: *"the sinful mind is hostile to God. It does not submit to God's law, nor can it do so."* Romans 8:7. Those whose mind is not on God have a bleak outlook: *"Their destiny is destruction, their god is their stomach, and their glory is in their shame. Their mind is on earthly things."* Philippians 3:19

So, let's get suited up. When we slip on our gear, we will be ready to play and we will feel like a million bucks. Do it now and enjoy it for a moment, because your opponent is out there, waiting for his opportunity to knock your helmet off!

Reading the Defense
"Your enemy the devil..." 1 Peter 5:8a

Underestimating the Challenge

I believe we men tend to minimize what it's going to take to make a marriage and family work. We drastically misjudge how much focus it requires to build a life-long, fulfilling relationship. I know that I was horribly unprepared for what I was about to face when Carol and I walked down the aisle. Just like that day in practice when I was hit by that safety, I wasn't ready, and I had no idea what was about to hit me.

Statistics are the language of sports. Fans relate to them, memorize, recite them, and base decisions on them. Depending on whom you listen to, or which survey you believe, roughly 50 percent of marriages are ending in divorce. That is a significant statistic. It presents a troubling and bleak picture. Couples don't walk down the aisle with a sense that they have just a 50 percent chance of making it. What happens along the way that makes marriage so difficult?

We do not consider how the enemy of our souls, the devil, does not want Christian men and women to live in harmony and holiness. I think he targets every man who calls himself by the name of the Son of God. He knows that failed marriages send a message to others that Christianity doesn't work!

The Devil Wants to Cripple Us
"Your enemy the devil prowls around like a roaring lion looking for someone to devour."
1 Peter 5:8b

I am a fan of Animal Planet, and the Discovery Channel. I love watching things like *When Big Cats Attack!* They show a leopard, lion, or a tiger crouching in the weeds, waiting… waiting, patiently waiting for the gazelle to get close enough. Carol hates these scenes; in fact, I have to change the channel when she is in the room. For me, however, the anticipation is captivating.

When a big cat chooses to makes its move, it is an impressive display of muscle, stealth, precision, and ferocity. The helpless prey tries to get away, to no avail. Victory comes swiftly in most cases.

I think Peter wanted to give us a picture of how fierce, malicious, and dreadful the devil is. He is waiting patiently, taking his time, letting us believe we are just fine, allowing us to relax, wanting us to let our guard down. Then, when he pounces, he can carry us off in his teeth.

Only we are not dead. He just owns us. He controls us. He wants us to surrender our will to his. The devil doesn't want to kill us, only to wound us. If we are hurt, bitter, or resentful then we can become more useful to him. We are now able to inflict pain and anguish on others as his assistants. That's what happens when he gets a foothold.

The Devil is Suited Up and Has His Eye on Us

I wish the enemy was as easy to spot as a player in an opponent's jersey. It would certainly make it easier to distinguish the good guys from the bad. He is actually in disguise: *"for Satan himself masquerades as an angel of light."* 2 Corinthians 11:14

It is critical that we understand our opponent and his intentions. In football, we would spend hours and hours watching film and studying our adversaries. As family quarterbacks, we are in training to combat the prince of darkness. He's got some skill.

One of my favorite segments on *NFL Films* shows a wide-eyed Chicago Bears middle linebacker, Mike Singletary, looking menacingly at the quarterback. I met Mike many years ago, and he is a fine man of faith. However, his look and demeanor as a football player are a great visual to remind us of how our enemy has his eyes wide open, looking at us in a malicious way.

"Put on the full armor of God so that you can take your stand against the devil's schemes." Ephesians 6:11b. That's right. The devil is scheming against us! He is plotting, planning, creating tactics to get us off our game. He knows us; he is familiar with our weaknesses. He will be relentless in his attack on us! Think: blitzes from all corners of the field, unyielding, persistent pressure.

"For our struggle is not against flesh and blood, but against the rulers, against the authorities, against the powers of this dark world and against the spiritual forces of evil in the heavenly realms." Ephesians 6:12. I'm a pretty practical guy; I don't see demons at every corner or in every circumstance. I do believe however, that there are unseen forces trying to hinder us from experiencing the peace and love of God that is in Christ.

The Devil's Game Plan
"The thief comes to kill, steal and destroy." John 10:10a

He wants to destroy our faith:
- Tempting us into sin: *"Jesus was led by the Spirit into the desert to be tempted by the devil."* Matthew 4:3
- Distracting us: *"let us throw off everything that hinders and the sin that so easily entangles us."* Hebrews 12:1b.

This is like getting us to watch the cheerleaders on the sideline instead of focusing on our game. When we take our eyes off the field, we are no longer engaged in the battle.

He wants to deceive us:

- Lies: *"When he (the devil) lies, he speaks his native language, for he is a liar and the father of lies."* John 8:44b
- False teaching: *"Satan himself masquerades as an angel of light."* 2 Corinthians 11:14b.
  When we read the headlines that question our skill, it undermines the confidence that is required to lead. (Trust me, I know firsthand.)

He wants to influence us:

- Rebellion: *"the spirit (the devil's) who is now at work in those who are disobedient."* Ephesians 2:2b
- Impairing our vision: *"The god of this age has blinded the minds of unbelievers, so that they cannot see the light of the gospel of the glory of Christ."* 2 Corinthians 4:4.
  Your opponent starts trash talking, and grabbing you in inappropriate places during a pile up. You will be tempted to retaliate. (This, too, I know personally.)

He wants to divide us:

It is not uncommon for star players to receive a lot of publicity. Their response to special treatment can quickly divide a locker room.

- Anger: *"Do not let the sun go down while you are still angry, and do not give the devil a foothold."* Ephesians 4:26b
- Envy: *"If you harbor bitter envy and selfish ambition in your hearts… such 'wisdom' does not come down from heaven but is earthly, unspiritual, of the devil."* James 3:14a, 15b

In following chapters, we will examine more of the devil's tactics to derail our lives. We will break down numerous strategies and maneuvers he uses to keep us from enjoying, *"life to the full,"* John 10:10b. We will discuss how to relinquish the control of our lives to the Holy Spirit and discover, *"The reason the Son of God appeared was to destroy the devil's work."* 1 John 3:8b

The Red Zone
"No discipline seems pleasant at the time, but painful. Later on, however, it produces a harvest of righteousness and peace for those who have been trained by it." Hebrews 12:11

There are days and seasons of life that are etched into our memory. They are burned deep within our souls where they act as milestones along our winding journey. Some of those markers are sweet. Others have more of a bitter taste. Those defining moments become a part of the testimony that God wants to build into each one of our lives.

The first two years we had spent in Phoenix were mixed with blessings and trauma. We had moved to this desert oasis to serve in full-time ministry. The desire of our hearts was to share the gospel, and use the platform the Lord had given us through athletics to win others to Christ. At the same time, we were involved in a marriage discipleship program that was focused on learning to live with each other in an understanding way.

In my efforts to try to love my wife as Christ loved the church, I was getting more and more resentful, hostile and out of control. On one hand, I was trying to save the world, and on the other, I was attempting to learn how to care for Carol and the kids. Torn between the two, I took out my rage on her. I was abusive physically, emotionally and spiritually.

I had no idea that our lives were about to change one September day in 1989. I was clueless that God was about to turn our lives inside out and that He would begin to build a testimony that He wanted us to share from coast to coast. Like getting my helmet ripped off in practice, I will never forget the deep impact that day had on us. Carol made the most courageous choice of her life to that point, or since.

She left me.

We had been fighting for days, which was a typical experience for us. She needed a break, so she left the kids with me and found refuge at a friend's house just south of Phoenix. I thought it was just for a day or two. I was scheduled to take a trip to California, and Carol wanted to switch cars and get the kids, who were three and one years old at the time. We met at a parking lot because she didn't trust me to handle this exchange with grace. As she loaded the kids up, I had no idea that I wouldn't see them again for weeks.

I didn't know where she went. When I returned from California, I expected to find everyone at home. Maybe she would finally be the "good little pastor's wife" she was supposed to be. That's exactly what I was thinking. I was trying to do everything I could, and it never seemed to be enough. I kept pointing the finger at her, and she wasn't having it anymore. No one was home, and I was outraged.

I raged for at least a week. I called everyone close to us to find out where Carol and the kids were. I screamed at each one of our loving friends. It's difficult to write this because the pain and sadness is still in my heart. I treated people so poorly. I said terrible things. I behaved like a fool, because I was a fool.

After I had vented my venom on anyone who would listen, I had to look in the mirror. It was time for me to face the truth. I decided that my flesh had been getting the best of me and it was time to turn the tide. I had read that fasting was a good way to get one's self under control, but I love to eat. This was going to be painful. I was really desperate to get my mind right, so my goal was three full days, no food, only water.

The Lord is true to His word when He said, *"You will seek me and find me when you seek me with all your heart."* Jeremiah 29:13.

Perhaps for the first time in my life as a believer, I sought him with my whole heart. I had lost the most precious part of my life and I was finally breaking. I was at the end of my strength, my fighting was over and I was beginning to surrender my will to the King of Kings.

It finally dawned on me that Carol didn't leave me because I was so loving, patient and kind. In fact, I have never seen a woman yet who left her husband because he was so much like Christ.

As it began to soak in that I was the cause of her leaving, my grief began to multiply. I realized I was facing the same shame and sorrow, much like King David experienced when he wrote, *"Create in me a pure heart, O God, and renew a steadfast spirit within me. Do not cast me from your presence or take your Holy Spirit from me. Restore to me the joy of your salvation and grant me a willing spirit, to sustain me."* Psalm 51:10-12

Over time, Carol received word that my heart was softening and that I was starting to break. She contacted me, and together we negotiated her return to our house. If I would move out, she would come back. I would be moving out for a short time to let her know that I was serious in my desire to restore trust and hope. I stayed in a friend's extra bedroom. It was an awful, humbling, and entirely necessary process. You will learn more about our restoration process later.

Since then, over the last twenty years, we have traveled coast to coast, telling our story of redemption to give hope to those in need. I am still troubled by the number of men who, after hearing what we went through, will challenge Carol on why she left me. "Did you really need to do that?" they will ask. "Couldn't there have been a better way?"

What is difficult to understand is that there are no perfect, textbook scenarios on how to create restoration. God knows exactly what each man needs to awaken his heart. He knows what it will take to get our attention.

What must happen for a person's heart to soften so that he becomes willing to surrender his spirit to the Spirit of God? It may take getting your helmet knocked off into the end zone to capture your attention. Only then will you buckle your chin strap. Are you ready for more?

Prayer

Lord Jesus, create in us a clean heart. Forgive us for being stubborn and hard-hearted. We surrender to you, Holy Spirit, fill us with patience, kindness and humility. Lead us in the way everlasting. Amen.

Chapter 2
Recruiting

We have all watched the videos of national letter of intent signing day: The young man sitting in the gymnasium, cameras rolling, four different university hats in front of him. With his decision, he will change the course of his life, the fate of the school he chooses, and the fates of those he rejects. He is celebrated or reviled for the choice he makes. Alumni of his new school love him. He is condemned by those he spurned. Lord help him if he is choosing between rival schools in certain parts of the country. Fans take all of this personally and some of them have been known to make life miserable for a football player who, in their minds, chooses poorly. There is a fine line between enthusiasm and lunacy. (See Harvey Updyke, the crazy Alabama fan who poisoned the trees at Toomer's corner in Auburn).

It amazes me to see how serious our world is about high school football. There are literally dozens of websites dedicated to monitoring the careers of athletes not even old enough to drive. Some of these sites are evaluating ninth graders. It's ridiculous! The pressure and expectation on these athletes is greater than it's ever been.

My experience, however, was the opposite of those five-star quarterbacks who could choose any school in the entire country. I walked on. No scholarship. No fanfare. No special signing day theatrics. Just an opportunity to compete. In fact, I was lucky to be invited to walk on. Not everyone gets that chance.

The one recruiting visit I made was an enlightening experience. My parents drove all night from my high school game in Cheyenne, Wyoming, to take me to Lincoln. We were exhausted when we got to the lounge where all the recruits were hanging out.

Young high school football players like me had come from all over the country, some of them decked out in leather and gold chains. The now legendary Nebraska Head Coach Tom Osborne said to one highly touted running back, "Barry Switzer didn't give you that jacket did he?" I about fell on the floor laughing. That was my introduction to Coach's fabulous sense of humor.

I do remember getting letters from most of the small schools in Nebraska. It felt really good to be wanted. I still have a box with all the correspondence, media guides, and school propaganda that was sent to me. It's hard to throw away those love letters!

I did have an awkward experience with a coach of one small college in eastern Nebraska. When I told him I would be walking on in Lincoln. He told me, "You will never play there!" He was so insistent he continued with, "I would pay you a thousand dollars for every minute you play for the Huskers." He hung up on me. I wish I could remember his name. He owes me a bunch of Benjamins.

The year I spent as a graduate assistant coach at Nebraska in 1986, was a real eye opener for me regarding the pressure and importance of recruiting. When the season ended, the assistant coaches spent the majority of their time on the road. After viewing the travel itineraries of our coaches, I couldn't believe how many cities a coach could cover in one week.

The coaches are graded on how well they recruited their specific regions. If a coach was not proficient at getting kids to sign, it could jeopardize his job. If coaches can't recruit, teams can't win. If teams don't win, schools don't make the bowl games. If schools don't make the bowl games, nationally recognizable colleges won't be seen on TV, and then it's hard to recruit... it's a vicious cycle.

It all starts with recruiting.

The Play: Accept Your Calling from the Creator
"...you are not your own. You were bought with a price."
1 Corinthians 6:19b-20a

Guess what? You are being recruited. Right now. By God! You are being sought, desired and coveted. You are a five-star prospect! You and all those you will influence in your lifetime are affected by the choice you make in this recruiting war.

The idea for this section came from a Kenny Luck Everyman Ministries Conference. Kenny spoke about the idea of us being recruited by two entities:

The Father, Son and Holy Spirit vs. the devil, our flesh and the culture. The following is my expansion of that concept.

- Your loyalty is wanted.
- Your heart is desired.
- Your effort is coveted.

Your choice of allegiance will determine the course of your life, your children's lives and your legacy.

- Your identity is at stake.
- Your character will be defined.
- Your belief will take shape.

What The Father is Offering
- **Eternal life**

   "For God so loved the world that he gave his one and only son, that whoever believes in him shall not perish but have eternal life." John 3:16

   This is perhaps the most over-used and under-appreciated scripture of all time. This verse is spoken so flippantly that it may have lost the depth of its meaning. For those of you who have kids, ask yourself; would you ever give up one of your kids for me? No, you wouldn't. Frankly, I wouldn't give up one of my kids for you, either. I don't love you that much.

   To realize that our heavenly father thinks so much of us that he would allow his perfect son to die is astonishing. He did this for a purpose. He has a goal in mind. There is a plan. Jesus is the ultimate recruiting inducement. The NCAA can't do anything about it.

   God's plan is to keep us from being separated from Him. Sin is the problem and He took care of that through Christ. Romans tells us that the gift of God is eternal life in Christ. Eternal life is a gift! No one else is capable of offering this enticement. It's better than a fancy car and a house for your parents.

- **Forgiveness**
  "In him we have redemption through his blood, the forgiveness of sins, in accordance with the riches of God's grace that he lavished on us with all wisdom and understanding." Ephesians 1:7

  Who else can offer this? The challenge is discovering how to accept and embrace this precious generosity. This incentive is one to take advantage of. When your fumbles and interceptions are not held against you, the fear of failure is gone.

  Because sin separates us from Him, He had to present the perfect offering. *"He is the atoning sacrifice for our sins, and not only for ours but also for the sins of the whole world."* 1 John 2:2. Yes, God is recruiting the whole world. You get to be His instrument to enlist everyone you influence. You become a starter from the very first day.

What Jesus is Offering
- **Abundant Life**
  "I have come that they may have life, and have it to the full." John 10:10b

  A life fully committed to Jesus will be fulfilling, complete and meaningful. It doesn't imply a life without trial and struggle. The believer can be confident in God's plans. *"'I know the plans I have for you,' declares the Lord. 'Plans to prosper you and not to harm you, plans to give you hope and a future.'"* Jeremiah 29:11. Victory is guaranteed. Read the back of the book. This is our slice of heaven, it's a fixed game.

- **Freedom**
  "If you hold to my teaching, you are really my disciples. Then you will know the truth and the truth will set you free." John 8:31b-32

  Though Jesus, we can be free from guilt and shame.

  Guilt—*"Therefore, there is now no condemnation for those who are in Christ Jesus."* Romans 8:1. The guilt that can cripple, debilitate, and keep us from pursuing the very best that we can be does not have to control us. Freedom from the fear of being replaced allows for incredible confidence. You will never get benched!

Shame—*"Anyone who trusts in him will never be put to shame."* Romans 10:11b. For those who believe and trust in Him, the powerful paralyzing force of shame cannot hold us captive. A man who functions free of shame is a dangerous combatant. He won't be embarrassed by interceptions, bad decisions or mistakes

- **Power**
  "Now to him who is able to do immeasurably more than all we ask or imagine, according to his power that is at work within us." Ephesians 3:20

  Our own imaginations cannot contain the courage, wisdom and influence that we can have in Christ. His strength will be manifested to the same degree that we surrender to him. This unlimited power is superior to any PED (performance enhancing drug). No pills or needles required.

What the Holy Spirit is Offering
- **Guidance**—
  "The mind controlled by the Spirit is life and peace." Romans 8:6b

  "...when he, the Spirit of truth comes, he will guide you into all truth." John 16:13a. The Holy Spirit will help us navigate pitfalls, tests and adversities that we all face in our daily lives. Having this advisor creates comfort and confidence in our spirits. This kind of "play calling" will make our offense unstoppable. When we tune into the Holy Spirit, we make clear decisive choices that lead our entire team to peace.

  Perhaps the greatest influence to mankind from the Holy Spirit is found in Galatians 5:22-23a where we find the fruits of the Spirit:

  Love has the power to *"...cover a multitude of sin."* 1 Peter 4:8b. "God demonstrates his own love for us in this: While we were still sinners, Christ died for us." Romans 5:8

  Joy is the authority that gave Christ the courage, strength and foresight to overcome the fear and pain of crucifixion. "Let us fix our eyes on Jesus, the author and perfecter of our faith, who for the joy set before him endured the cross." Hebrews 12:2a

Peace gives us the power to conquer the burdens we encounter. "Cast all your anxiety on him because he cares for you." 1 Peter 5:7

Patience is the capacity to not been in control of the circumstances of your life, and be content with it. "A patient man has great understanding." Proverbs 14:29

Kindness is demonstrated in God's willingness to distribute his abundant grace to us in-spite of our sinfulness. "...by his wounds we were healed." 1 Peter 2:24b

Goodness God is good. He protects us and provides for all our needs. "For the Lord God is a sun and shield; the Lord bestows favor and honor; no good thing does he withhold from those that love him." Psalm 84:11

Faithfulness God is constant, unceasing in his care and the fulfillment of his promises. "But the Lord is faithful and he will strengthen and protect you from the evil one." 2 Thessalonians 3:3

Gentleness is the ability to restore and redeem with tenderness. "You give me your shield of victory, and your right hand sustains me; you stoop down to make me great." Psalm 18:35

Self-control is the power to deny, resist and stand against my flesh's desire. "For God did not give us a spirit of timidity, but a spirit of power, of love and of self-discipline." 2 Timothy 1:6

The Trinity makes a great recruiting pitch, just like the coach who makes a plea for your playing skills in service to the team. The Lord is knocking, making His case, giving you options, showing you the advantages of turning your life to Him. *"Those that trust in the Lord will find new strength. They will soar high on wings like eagles."* Isaiah 40:31

Reading the Defense
"Resist the devil and he will flee from you."
James 4:7

The Devil, the head of the "Axis of Evil," WANTS YOU! He wants your flesh, and he conspires with the culture to gain your allegiance. Together, they will do whatever it takes to keep you from your calling. We want to examine the work of these forces to hold you back from the life that you were created to enjoy. There is a battle for the control of your mind, spirit and behavior. The victor will direct your life and your legacy.

What the Devil is Selling
- **Deception**

    "...for there is no truth in him (the devil). When he lies, he speaks his native language, for he is a liar and the father of lies." John 8:44b

    It started in the beginning with the Garden of Eden. Adam and Eve were enjoying their calling. The devil comes along for his first recruiting visit. He sits with his prey and weaves his deceit. He mixes a little truth with his lie, like a drop of poison in a glass of pure water. It seems innocent in the beginning and ends with bitterness.

    From the story in Genesis 3 the devil says to Eve *"Did God really say, 'You must not eat from any tree in the garden?'"* He starts by creating a question that gets Eve off balance; you will see this tactic from your flesh and the culture as well. Eve answers with truth: *"We may eat fruit from the trees in the garden, but God did say, 'You must not eat fruit from the tree that is in the middle of the garden, and you must not touch it, or you will die.'"* Genesis 3:2b-3

    This is where the enemy of our soul entices us, and we start to have a debate or conversation with him. He is good at his craft and knows how to lure us into his reasoning, as he did with Eve. *"You will not surely die,"* the devil says to Eve. *"For God knows that when you eat of it your eyes will be opened, and you will be like God, knowing good and evil."* Genesis 3:4-5. There is truth in this statement, hiding the fact that the death would be spiritual not physical. I'm not certain Eve knew what *death* meant. The devil wants us to question God's Word and His motives in our life.

    The results of this recruiting visit created Satan's greatest weapon in the debilitation of the human race: Shame.

- **Shame**

  "I was afraid because I was naked." Genesis 3:10

  After eating the fruit in which they were commanded not to, Adam and Eve hid. Guilt and shame of sin drove them into darkness. The weapon of shame is used with malicious intent to create isolation, fear and insecurity. Once shame takes root, it can choke out the Spirit and drag the family quarterback into darkness. *"My disgrace is ever before me all day long, and my face is covered with shame."* Psalm 44:15

Now that the devil had his first human recruits, Adam and Eve, they birthed sin into the entire race. Later, he set his sights on the Son of God himself. The devil's pitch involved a forty-day visitation in the desert to tempt Jesus into switching teams. His strategy included the use of scripture to get the Lord off balance; you will also see this tactic used against you! Unable to turn Jesus against the Father, the devil then turned to human nature to conspire against mankind.

What the Flesh is Offering
"... one is tempted when, by his own evil desire,
he is dragged away and enticed." James 1:14

- **Slavery**

  The flesh loves to enjoy itself. It knows no boundaries and it has an unquenchable thirst. The trap is tricking us into trying to fulfill its desires. It cannot be satisfied. It won't be gratified; there is no end to its need. Eventually, your life is not your own. Your flesh is now the ruler of your world and you just follow its every whim. *"The evil deeds of a wicked man ensnare him; the cords of his sin hold him fast."* Proverbs 5:22. It's like having to be an Oklahoma Sooner for life... Sorry Sooner fans, I just had to say it.

- **Impotence**

  When speaking about the flesh, the usual topic is sexual purity. We all know that the use of pornography is a plague upon the people of God. The flesh wants to drag us into depravity without disclosing the cost. Proverbs 5 is a warning against immorality and the consequences of allowing ourselves to be trapped by lust. "*Keep to a path far from her* (the prostitute), *do not go near the door of her house* (the Internet), *lest you give your best strength to others*" Proverbs 5:8a. When we allow our lower human nature to direct our steps into submission to a prostitute or to pornography, we surrender our "*best strength*" to them. We give up our power for a temporary sexual fix. Without our strength, we are rendered ineffective and inadequate.

- **Poverty**

  Proverbs 5 goes on to reveal that sexual immorality will not only take your power it will also take your cash. "...*lest strangers feast on your wealth and your toil enrich another man's house.*" Proverbs 5:10. In the margin of my Bible, I wrote "Hugh Hefner," to remind me that if I indulge in *Playboy*, he is the one profiting from my sin. Proverbs also tells us that if we follow our own desires, our financial well-being will be passed on to others, "...*but a sinner's wealth is stored up for the righteous*" Proverbs 13:22b

- **Death**

  "*For the wages of sin is death,*" Romans 6:23a

  As we choose whom we will serve, the ultimate penalty for our misplaced allegiance is death. This death is disguised with the false promise of happiness and the facade of love. "*There is a way that seems right to a man, but in the end it leads to death.*" Proverbs 16:25. This death may not necessarily be physical or permanent. This death can manifest itself emotionally in separation from those we love.

If the devil is ineffective in securing our services, and if our flesh is not gaining traction in our life, then the world is there to distract, provoke and entice us. The devil knows he is losing the game, but he is still going to try and take out your ACL if he can.

What the Culture is Offering
"Do not love the world or anything in the world." 1 John 2:15a

- **The Lie that God is Powerless or Doesn't Care**
  How can all the suffering and calamities of this world happen if there is a truly loving God? How can you explain famine, floods, hurricanes, rape, incest, murder, infertility, genocide, etc.? If he or she or whatever is omnipotent, omniscient, and omnipresent how could this all-power being possibly stand by and witness all this? *"The fool says in his heart, 'There is no God.'"* Psalm 14:1a. When we believe there is no God, we won't turn to the Creator for help, guidance and grace.

- **Worship of Other Gods**
  We all remember the story of Moses: the mountain, a burning bush, the Ten Commandments, and then the people grew impatient and made a golden calf to worship. Since *"...there is nothing new under the sun."* Ecclesiastes 1:9b, is it possible that we have created our own images to worship instead of waiting for God? Not only is it possible, it is actually the greatest threat to our devotion.

  What is worship anyway? Isn't it a dedication of time, energy and focus? Can we actually measure what is important to us by the amount of time spent cultivating it? We have established idols, icons and false gods that consume our lives and distract us from the Creator himself. Don't believe me? Consider the list that follows:

  Money—We don't think we idolize money. Yet, ask yourself how much debt are you in? How long will it take to get out of that debt? How has that debt changed the way you live your life? Don't forget that, "the borrower is servant to the lender." Proverbs 22:7b

  Power—Working our way up the corporate ladder, trying to be the most successful salesman in our region, building our real estate business, or just trying to get that promotion? Why? What is motivating our striving? Let's face it: What we do and how much we make doing it create a part of our identity, security and influence. "Do not wear yourself out to get rich." Proverbs 23:4a

Entertainment—We need to ask ourselves this question: How much time do we spend watching football, golf, tennis, fishing, the Olympics, or *Duck Dynasty*? If you are like me, you know that too many hours evaporate in front of the television. Our culture is focused on worshiping performers; we even call it *American Idol.* We fill stadiums, buy jerseys, raise our voices, and pay thousands of dollars in devotion to modern icons. *"You shall have no other gods before me. You shall not make for yourself an idol in the form of anything in heaven above or on the   earth beneath or in the waters below. You shall not bow down to them or worship them"* Exodus 20:3-5a. This is the first commandment handed down to Moses. In an effort to break our daily habit of TV viewing. I simply unplugged it for a long season of our life. This was one of the most profitable choices we ever made. I dare you to try it!

Of course, this is not a comprehensive list of the devices that the devil, the flesh and our culture will use to keep us from worshiping the one and only true God. Throughout this book, we will examine the extensive ways our enemy tries to thwart or hinder our faith, distract us from truth and enlist us in his roster of victims.

The Red Zone
"All this I will give you" the devil said to Jesus.
Matthew 4:9a

The enemy of our souls will continue to recruit us until we die. He doesn't give up. Too many times in my life I have given in to his lies and deception. Daily we get to make choices. Those decisions may dictate the course of our lives. The following story was defining opportunity for me to choose Jesus.

Even though we won the Sugar Bowl at the end of my junior year, the season ended with great disappointment for me personally. Little did I know that following the game, my greatest temptation and victory was about to set the trajectory of my future.

We ended up playing in the Sugar Bowl because I performed poorly and we lost to Oklahoma. It was a painful defeat because we would have had a chance to play for the national title. My buddy, senior Craig Sundberg, outplayed me in the Oklahoma game, so he was named the starter for the bowl game against Louisiana State University.

The Sugar Bowl is played at the Super Dome in downtown New Orleans. The city is a mixture of cultures, cuisines and worldly enticements. It was a fascinating experience for a group of small-town Nebraska boys. We spent many evenings walking around the famous French Quarter. Several of us brought our Bibles to proselytize the patrons of the many unique establishments. We debated religion with a group of Hari Krishna's, shared the Gospel with strangers and even inadvertently wandered into a homosexual establishment. We ate dinner at one of the finest restaurants I had ever been to, and right across the street was a drag queen bar. Every sin, enticement, and temptation was right there within a two-block radius.

During the week in New Orleans, Craig and I had several chances to share our faith publicly. Newspaper and television interviews along with the Fellowship of Christian Athletes banquet gave us a platform to bring praise to Jesus. I was grateful for the opportunities we were given, and we tried to make the most of them. All of these proclamations of faith would eventually be tested.

Every mountain top has a valley. I was living "the dream" and the testing and trials of the valley were inevitable. My struggles started early in the week with a message from Carol. She was in Urbana, Illinois, for a missions conference. To this point, I had proposed marriage on three separate occasions, and been rebuffed each time. Her message on the telegram was, "Please pray for me." She had been considering a mission trip to Australia, so that meant to me, "I'm leaving. Our relationship is over." I was devastated.

To add to my misery, I threw an interception in my only appearance in the first half of the game. I played a little at the end when the game was out of reach. Craig played great and was named the game's MVP, which was a fitting end to a difficult year for him. I was very proud of how he played and glad he was honored in that way. He deserved it. My relationship with Craig became one of the most significant blessings of my career.

After the game was over, I was left with no fiancé, another poor performance and an uncertain future. I had my jersey in hand, and a Walkman cassette player. Instead of taking the bus with the team, I decided to walk the mile back to the Hilton Hotel. I needed time alone.

In my vulnerable condition, the evil recruiter made a visit. The devil, my flesh and New Orleans started to pull me toward the French Quarter. Every sin imaginable was right there, just a couple of blocks away. The thoughts started to flood my mind, Satan made his pitch, "You can get sex, let's find some drugs, nobody will ever know. You can at least get a little drunk, you deserve it, nobody cares about you, nobody will know. Let's just go see what's over there, take a look, nobody will ever know. Carol is gone, you sucked tonight, nobody will know. You know you are not much of a Christian, you are a phony, nobody will know. Who do you think you are? It will be good for you, nobody will know, nobody will know, nobody will know..." I was being lured and enticed and the pitch was convincing. I had a choice to make, and nobody would know.

I had a Leon Patillo song turned up on my Walkman to drown out the lies, deceit and antagonism. I was jamming to my favorite tune "J.E.S.U.S," a song that would be a big hit at my wedding to Carol in just eight months. The lyrics start with "J.E.S.U.S, he's my Lord and King, J.E.S.U.S he's my everything."

I set my eyes on the road ahead, kept my head down, and I made my choice; a choice that would need to be made thousands of times in my life. A choice to follow Christ. A choice to resist the devil. A choice to discipline myself. A choice to turn from the world. A choice to let the Spirit of God comfort me, strengthen me, and give me hope. A choice that I have never regretted.

Prayer

Dear Jesus, I choose you today. Come into my life. Forgive me of my sin. Strengthen me in my battle. I give you my life today. You are my Lord. You are my savior. I choose Christ. Amen.

CHAPTER 3
THE PLAYBOOK

The first couple of days of fall camp my freshman year in 1981 were spent standing around in gym shorts. The team was herded through physical exams, weight-ins, measurements and the dreaded "turn your head and cough" routine. The process is dehumanizing, really. It reminds me of a cattle roundup.

Immediately I discovered that I was one of many prospects who had been working most of their lives to make it in a program like this. In that moment, I realized that my dream was close at hand but it was going to take a lot of work to be fulfilled. For me it was the first real gut check of my career. I had already asked myself, "Do I have what it takes?" The pressure, intensity and anxiety are noticeable but unspoken.

What I remember of those days was how large everyone seemed to be. I was six three and weighed 200 pounds, so I wasn't small by any stretch. In fact, I was the largest guy on my high school team. Compared to most of these guys, I felt puny. I found it difficult not to notice my teammates and to feel a little intimidated. I recall thinking, "that dude's legs are huge!" If I was going to succeed, I would have to set aside all my insecurities and act as if I belonged, even though everything inside of me said, "You are in way over your head." Faking confidence can become a way of life. This is where that process really got tested for me.

After the initial measuring and weigh-in, the next item on the agenda was to go to position meetings. We quarterbacks were introduced to our freshman quarterback coach and to our playbook. Jeff Quinn was our QB coach, a responsibility he was given after finishing his playing career, He was refreshingly humble and kind. He was also a detail person. When I was younger, I had watched him play on TV several times. Now he was my coach. This was sweet!

Jeff made it clear that our responsibilities extended beyond our playing positions. We were told that we must have a thorough understanding of not only our position, but also every other position on the field. We were required to know what every player was expected to do. For example, if you as the quarterback call a play in the huddle and the right guard looks to you for help because he doesn't quite understand his responsibility in the play, you need to tell him who to block. It was up to the quarterback to keep everyone on the same page.

We received our playbook. It was enormous, filled with diagrams, sets, defenses, adjustments and terminology I had never heard before. It was like studying the phone book. I felt a sinking feeling in the pit of my stomach and shuddered. How in the world was I going to comprehend all this?

It was like learning a foreign language. We needed to understand all aspects of the offense thoroughly. We had came from across the nation where we all had learned and operated different offenses on our high school teams. We needed to relearn everything. On top of that, we were competing with one another for playing time. There were six quarterbacks on the freshman team. We all wanted to play. Each of us had to look around and believe that he was better than the next guy. At least I wasn't the only one looking a little dazed by it all.

The goal was to understand the playbook so well that we wouldn't have to think, just react. If you had to think, it was too late. The college game is too fast to allow for hesitation. The greatest players know exactly what they are supposed to do on every play.

The coach told us we would also have to be familiar with defensive formations. We would need to be able to recognize defensive adjustments and what would or wouldn't work against each defense. We also learned that those defensive formations would change week to week with each opponent, so it was our responsibility to understand their personnel and what their strengths and weaknesses were.

After being given this enormous task, we were offered the option to change positions if we did not believe we could handle the expectations set before us. There were no takers. Each one of us believed he was "the man."

I remember taking the field for our first scrimmage my freshman year. I was lost and extremely nervous. Okay, I was scared to death. During each play, I recall trying to remember at least five different things. My head was spinning and I'm certain I turned the wrong way at least three times. The cameras were recording our plays that afternoon, so we knew we would be watching our mistakes the next day. That added to the stress. I had no self-confidence and it showed. I was fourth string at this point.

I was overwhelmed, confused, and scared. I was afraid that I could never fully grasp all of this information. I studied all the time. When we weren't practicing, I was memorizing the playbook and walking through the footwork.

The amazing thing was how we practiced. Every day we took one concept or play and worked on it until it became natural. We would run the same play over and over again. Then we would run it again just to make certain we got it right. Every day, day after day.

Practice Creates Confidence

By the spring of 1984, I knew the playbook inside and out. I understood the offense and the defense, and I appreciated what was required. I took the field with a confidence that came from practice and experience, but mostly from a thorough grasp of our offense. That confidence is what allowed me to play with authority. It ultimately earned me a scholarship.

As I progressed, I began to understand my roles and responsibilities with greater clarity. With that came the confidence that helped me overcome my physical limitations. Since I was a walk on, not much was expected of me. Every year, new quarterbacks joined the program with more talent than I had. After injuries set me back during my first two playing seasons, my opportunity to make the starting team finally came the spring before my junior year.

Note: If you would like to see an actual Nebraska playbook from the old days, here is the link: http://www.footballxos.com/download/offense/college-offense/1983-Nebraska-Offense.pdf

The Play: Know the Word of God

"I have hidden your word in my heart that I might not sin against you."
Psalm 119:11

Like a football playbook, the Bible can be a little intimidating. Actually, it can be overwhelming when you start to study it. There are varying perspectives about scripture including things like which version to read, how to interpret it, and what books are really important. Some wonder where to begin. The major consideration is: Do you trust the Word of God? It is imperative to ask ourselves this question, because how we approach scripture, will determine how we apply it to our lives.

It troubles me that theologians who study this document from the original languages and every conceivable angle don't necessarily agree on it. All denominations, factions and cults are built around their own particular interpretations of scripture. Instead of bringing people closer together and closer to God, conflicting interpretations of this document have divided the people of God for centuries. Nevertheless, I cannot allow that to keep me from being a student of the Bible. I'm still learning and I'm never going to stop.

I would love it if someone just told me exactly what everything in the Bible is supposed to mean, especially for me personally. But that is not how it works. The Bible is designed for us to use in our daily experience to help us. Ultimately, it takes revelation by the Holy Spirit for me to apply the word correctly in my life. It is intended to be held in our spirit while being comprehended in our mind.

At some point we have to put all the doubts, fears and confusion about the usefulness of the Bible behind us. Leaning and applying The Bible is essential for the family quarterback who is striving for godliness. Like a quarterback who yearns to understand his offense, so does the man of God thirst to comprehend the word.

The Bible is Your Playbook

We husbands and fathers are the family quarterback and the Bible is our playbook. We need to know it; we need to understand it, and we must allow it to be part of who we are. Will this happen quickly? NO. But, that's okay. The game of life is a journey and right now is the perfect time for us to commit to learning our playbook.

Hebrews 4:12 gives us a little insight into using this dynamic and divinely inspired work of art; "*The word of God is living and active. Sharper than any double-edged sword, it penetrates even to dividing soul and spirit, joints and marrow; it judges the thoughts and attitudes of the heart.*" God invites us to study the word so that He can join us on our journey. It is a part of His grace to provide testimony of those who have gone before us. In the Bible, we read stories of imperfect saints whose lives demonstrate God's mercy and provision.

Let's look a little more closely at what Hebrews says about the word of God:

- **Living**

  Scripture takes on a life of its own. This is why two people can read a passage and come up with two different ways to look at it. Because it's alive. It can grow within us. How we understand it will evolve with our faith. It is not stagnant.

  I have enjoyed observing how a verse will have an impact on me in a certain way, then years later, the same verse affects me entirely differently. For example when I was in college I read Proverbs 16:25 *"There is a way that seems right to a man, but in the end it leads to death."* That verse meant, if you live a life of self-gratification you will end up dying in the gutter. After I got married and I struggled with how to demonstrate love for Carol, it began to mean that having to be right would end with her crying, being sad and extremely discouraged. Now, with the understanding that I have today, that is what the description of death means to me.

- **Active**

  In the Greek, the word "active" (energes) means effective, energized and powerful. It has the ability to change us, if we will allow it to. One illustration is Proverbs 5. It is a warning against adultery. This chapter has given me strength and resilience to battle the temptations that come from pornography and a culture that flaunts immorality.

As we permit the principles of scripture to influence our thinking, our ideas and attitudes will be shaped. Our perspectives and how we view the world around us will be altered.

First and Foremost, The Bible is For YOU

One of the major criticisms I have of Christians today, is that we tend to try to apply God's Word to everyone else and not to ourselves. That is called hypocrisy. This has been a major struggle for me personally, as I will share later. I believe that this is a legitimate concern that we need to consider.

We will talk about leading by example in a later chapter. As the family quarterback, God's word is for us! We need to apply it in our own lives and the rest will follow. *"All scripture is God-breathed and is useful for teaching, rebuking, correcting and training in righteousness, so that the man of God may be thoroughly equipped for every good work."* 2 Timothy 3:16-17

God's playbook provides all the information that I need to be successful:

- **Teaching**

  The Bible is instruction for living a right life; a road map to wisdom. It's the game plan. Let God's playbook be our guide. Let's review it daily.

- **Rebuking**

  Sometimes we need to be convinced of the discrepancies between our own behavior and what the Bible describes as godliness. There is value in realizing that the Creator understands how to have success. Verses of scripture are like the coach who gives you a little push in the right places.

- **Correcting**

  Often in our lives we get off course, and it takes a little nudge to get us back on the path that leads to life. It helps us to see our opponent and how our adversary is influencing us. On the field, during practice, we would have coaches show us the proper technique to help us be more precise. The Word can have this same effect.

- **Training in Righteousness**

  Since none of us is righteous, we need to discover what that looks like. A strategy for success: *"For physical training is of some value, but godliness has value for all things, holding promise for both the present life and the life to come."* 1 Timothy 4:8. When your objective is the perfect execution of every play, success typically follows.

Time to Study

"Do your best to present yourself to God as one approved, a workman who does not need to be ashamed and who correctly handles the word of truth." 2 Timothy 3:16-17

Comprehending the word of God is not going to happen quickly or completely in this lifetime. Since God's Word is living and active, we can trust that it will consistently have an effect on our world if I we continue to study it. It is up to us to dedicate ourselves to understanding it.

God's word, the sword of the Spirit, is the last piece of your equipment that prepares you for the battle. Our dedication to comprehension will enhance our ability to apply God's ways in our life.

What are we willing to commit to?

- **Daily Study:** Can we start by spending ten minutes a day in study? Let our love for study grow.

- **Weekly Discussions:** Can we meet with other men to read scripture and discuss its application? This has great value. Gathering with other men is like a team meeting to discuss a game plan with tactical strategy. We grow stronger together. We are waging war against the kingdom of darkness. Don't underestimate the opponent.

- **Depth vs. Distance:** I prefer to read the Bible in a manner that allows me to grasp the deeper principles and concepts. If that means just reading one chapter, or even one verse in a sitting, that's not a problem. Understanding the nuances of an intricate pass play may take lots and lots of time. So, too, will the weighty things of God. We ran the same plays so many times back when I was learning the playbook, I can do them in my sleep to this day. I can relate to the Saying of Agur in Proverbs 30: 2-3, *"I am the most ignorant of men; I do not have a man's understanding. I have not learned wisdom, nor have I knowledge of the Holy One."*

- **Consistency:** As the body needs nourishment throughout the day, our spirits have the same need, a hunger for righteousness and a thirst for truth. It is critical that I feed my heart (spirit) what it longs for. *"Like newborn babies, crave pure spiritual milk, so that by it you may grow up in your salvation, now that you have tasted that* *the Lord is good."* 1 Peter 2:2-3. We practiced, studied and reviewed film daily. We memorized our plays, defenses and strategy.

Confidence

I am a firm believer in the principle of reaping and sowing. We will talk about this constantly throughout this book. *"Do not be deceived: God cannot be mocked. A man reaps what he sows."* Galatians 6:7. It is our responsibility to create habits of consistent study, meditation and practice.

The net result for a player who knows his playbook is confidence. He has a thorough understanding of his roles and responsibilities. When he is equipped with a clear grasp of scripture, the man of God can walk through the trials of life with incredible assurance, with confidence, and with security and faith. There is no defense that can stand a chance against a man who knows his playbook.

Reading the Defense
"...my people are destroyed from lack of knowledge"
Hosea 4:6a

An entire book could be written about the things that keep us from reading and understanding God's Word. I believe that most Christians realize the importance of biblical understanding and awareness, yet, when you ask men how often they ready the Bible, they typically say, "Not enough." To me this means, "Not really at all."

As a player, understanding the playbook was essential and I could not survive without a thorough grasp of it. I think this is true for the believer as well. We must hunger for a greater understanding of the Word. Without it, we are like a ship with no compass. How will we find our way to where we ultimately want to be? Over the years I have watched many men prosper and many fall away in their faith and marriages. The key component has always been a man's dedication to personal application of scripture.

This is precisely why the devil does not want us to read the Bible. He desires to keep us in the dark, directionless, frustrated, and lost. A man must be willing to overcome the obstacles Satan himself places in our way to keep us from spending time consistently reading the Word.

- **Time**

  The first obstacle I struggle with when it comes to investing time in studying scripture is...I'M TOO BUSY. We are inundated with distractions throughout the day. It seems like we have less margin in our lives than ever before. Never in the history of the world have we been so connected with each other (social media), consumed with information (web news, blogs, etc.) and instantly entertained (YouTube).

  With these kinds of distractions, I doubt there is a time in our day when we would be prompted to spontaneously pick up our Bible. The enemy of our soul does not want us to do that. We have a thousand alternatives and opportunities (productive procrastination) just to keep us out of the Bible.

  The devil knows this "Good Book" really is good! He knows it can change us. He fears our use of it. He knows we are dangerous when we read it, much like someone using a sword. Without it, we are like a football player turning the wrong way, confused and waiting to be hit.

  Since we have only twenty-four hours in our day and because we sleep roughly six to eight of those hours, the devil only has to keep us distracted for the other sixteen hours to be effective. Sometimes I think it is a game he is trying to play with me. Even as I have been writing this book, he has found ways to keep me from the keyboard. He is creative, enticing and malevolent. His schemes are ancient and well-tested. They have worked for thousands of years. In twenty-first century America, Satan has at his disposal a plethora of misdirection to keep us from our playbook.

- **Energy**

  Are you tired, weary and exhausted from a burdensome life? Perfect! That is exactly where the devil wants you to be. We are running around like a freshman, not knowing what hit us. We do not know which way is up. We are so busy going to meetings, to events and even to church, that we don't have the energy to read or even listen to God's word.

As I have grown older, my stamina has diminished considerably. That makes me more aware that I sometimes think we are literally trying to run ourselves into the ground. When there are seasons in our life that offer us no down time, recovery or rest, I think this plays right into Satan's hands.

I know that if I am too tired and weary, the devil has a much greater influence on my attitude. If I am too worn out to fill my spirit up with the word of God, my spirit runs empty and I have nothing to give. Like a quarterback whose shoulder is injured, I can't complete a pass. I becomes useless.

Physical and spiritual fatigue can cause us to become less effective in all areas of our life. It's like a defense that blitzes every play. It wears you out. It gets you off balance and causes you to make mistakes.

By the fourth quarter, a team can get so worn down it just don't function well anymore. I remember watching the Seattle Seahawks completely take the steam out of the Denver Broncos in Super Bowl XLVIII. Perhaps the greatest offense in the history of the NFL was demoralized by relentless pressure.

- **Entertainment**

We live in a world of instant gratification and amusement. When we are not focused on earning a living, we tend to try and find things that create a distraction from our daily grind. From social media, YouTube, and television, to *World of Warcraft, Madden NFL* and *Farmville,* there is a never-ending array of time-killing, mind-numbing, worthless endeavors to steal our life from us.

I know that sounds kind of harsh, but it's true. I'm just as guilty as anybody else is when it comes to wasting time with recreation. The trouble is not the use of entertainment, but the lack of balance that can snatch hours from our lives. Have you ever squandered an hour on funny YouTube videos? Me too. I know a few guys who have no problem losing a night's sleep to play *Call of Duty.*

Technology has made amusement even more accessible. Yes, I too have found myself lost in a quest to reach another level of *Angry*

Birds. I am so easily addicted to that kind of activity that I had to delete those apps from my phone. It's as if I hear them calling to me "Come on, Travis, let's have some fun. I know you can do better than last time." I read a blog the other day about a man getting a divorce. It wasn't from his wife; it was from his phone, a device his spouse called "his mistress."

- **Hobbies**

  I love to have fun. I love to compete, drive fast, and do anything that can get my heart rate going. Most men have things in their lives that make them feel alive. These pastimes are important to a man's health and wellbeing. They also can be the obsessions that lead to disconnection and, if they are not careful, to divorce.

  We can be junkies for this kind of stuff. I know guys who can spend hours and hours taking an engine apart, cleaning them, scrubbing, polishing, and putting it all back together again. This gives them a rush. Working into the late hours tinkering on a project, losing track of time, totally immersed. Investing hours and days into what? What is the net result? What will we reap when we sow into pastimes?

  One of my loves is golf. I'm not a very good golfer, I just love to play and compete. Throw in a good cigar and it's pretty much heaven on earth for me. The problem is the five hours it takes to play eighteen holes, hundreds of dollars in equipment and the lost Benjamins in greens fees. Add to that the nasty attitude I get when I play poorly and this piece of paradise becomes miserable for everyone around me. That is, until I schedule another round. Then I need to practice. I need to get a new putter ($$$). I need better balls ($$$). As you can see, this can become a vicious cycle.

  The devil's goal is to thrill us, consume us, distract us and get us to become passionate about anything but Jesus. Then we will be fulfilling the godlessness described in 2 Timothy 3:2a-5a *"People will be lovers of themselves...lovers of pleasure rather than lovers of God—having a form of godliness but denying its power."*

The Red Zone

"Do your best to present yourself to God as one approved"
2 Timothy 2:15a

I will never be accused of being a scholar. I was in the fourth of the class that made the upper three-quarters possible. I have been running from the "dumb jock" label my whole life. I am scatterbrained, and I like to make up words that really embarrass my wife. I do however, have a fascination with the Bible. I have been reading God's word since my junior year in high school when I was given my first Bible. It was at that time that I asked Jesus into my life and I have been a student ever since. To this day I know a lot of verses, just don't ask me for the addresses.

The problem for me came when I started reading scripture to develop speeches, sermons and antidotes to help other people. I would be reading and I would underline something and then write a name next to it in my Bible—the name of someone whom I thought needed to hear it. I would find great stories to encourage, inspire and challenge everyone but me. As a result, a terrible thing started to happen. I got full of myself, and I didn't even know it.

The height of my arrogance was revealed during the early years of my marriage. I tell you this with terrible regret and a heap of shame. I used my knowledge of scripture as a weapon against my wife all the time. I would tell her what she was supposed to do and support it with God's word. I would berate her, accuse her, and humiliate her with scripture. Even now, I ask Jesus to forgive me for this terrible indiscretion.

As I became more and more spiritually abusive, she pulled away more and more until she finally left. It took weeks of her being gone and a three-day fast for me to hear Jesus say, "She didn't leave you because you are so peaceful, patient, and kind!" That should seem pretty obvious, yet I was so full of self-righteousness that I couldn't see it through my justification and piety. I had become the man described in 1 Corinthians 8:1b-3: *"Knowledge puffs up, but love builds up. The man who thinks he knows something does not yet know as he ought to know."*

A Game-changing Vision

When Carol was gone, I got so depressed about what I had done, I really wanted to die. I realized I had thrown away the best thing that had ever happened to me. I thought my life was over. I started shopping for a gun. I figured my family was better off without me.

During this time, I had a dream. I was standing before Jesus. He was bright, shining like the sun. And He welcomed me. There was joy in my heart. Then I realized there was a figure standing next to me that I couldn't identify. It was charred, burnt and unrecognizable. I looked at Jesus and asked Him "What is that?" He said, "That is the spirit of the wife I gave you." Then He asked me a question that sobered me up. "Do you still think you can get in (to heaven)?"

Without going into a theological discussion about eternal salvation or predestination, I have to tell you, I was scared. The game for me had started to change. I knew right then that I needed to start focusing my biblical understanding on myself. My energy and intent had to become about knowing Jesus, not merely knowing about Jesus. The verses needed to become life to my spirit and direction for my life. In order for me to restore my marriage, I needed to start following the advice of Matthew 6:33: *"But, seek first his kingdom and his righteousness and all these things will be given to you as well."*

Reading Scripture For my Own Need

I began reading with a sense of urgency. I was thirsty for insight, wisdom and hope. I was also afraid of myself. I didn't trust my thinking, attitudes and actions. My perspectives had destroyed everything that I loved. I needed the word just to live. My ways had caused death to my marriage.

My study took on a whole new life. I literally got up in the morning and grabbed my Bible as though it was a life raft. I became singularly focused on fixing me. I needed grace, I needed peace, I needed mercy and I found it in the pages between Genesis and Revelation. I found a Holy Father who loves me no matter what. *"I am convinced that neither the present nor the future, nor any power, neither height nor depth, nor anything else in all creation, will be able to separate us from the love of God that is in Christ Jesus our Lord."* Romans 8:38

I discovered that God could use me, the most immoral of men, to do His will (see King David's story in the Books of Samuel). I began to understand that God wanted to transform my life from the destruction it was into a new place that honors Him. It's much like the story of how Joseph went from the pit and the prison to the palace in the book of Genesis. I found strength in the apostles who were flawed, much like me (see Peter's denial). I found there was hope for me, too.

Confidence that Comes from Knowledge

Just like knowing my playbook, for me to understand the love, grace and mercy that pours from scripture transformed my arrogance into a broken confidence that would allow me to rebuild my family's lives. *"If my people, who are called by my name, will humble themselves and pray and seek my face and turn from their wicked ways, then will I hear from heaven and will forgive their sin and will heal their land."* 2 Chronicles 7:14. God can heal our marriages, if we choose to let His word transform us.

Prayer

Dear Jesus, forgive us for our pride and selfishness. Let your word strengthen us, inspire us, convict us and change us. Guide us as we read The Bible, your gift to humanity. Allow us to use it rightly, to encourage and build one another up. May it direct our paths and keep us from the evil one. Amen.

CHAPTER 4
THE SNAP

The first offensive play of Super Bowl XLVIII set the tone for the entire game. Some have said that this play actually caused the demise of the greatest offense in NFL history. This historic play was a blown snap.

The most basic action taken by any offense went awry when center Manny Ramirez hiked the ball over Peyton Manning's shoulder while Manning was barking out orders to the offense. He was at the line of scrimmage. Luckily, running back Knowshon Moreno managed to chase down the ball in the end zone, where he limited the damage to a safety. This was the fastest score in Super Bowl history: twelve seconds. The Denver Broncos never seemed to recover and they lost 43-8 to the Seattle Seahawks.

In football, everything starts with the snap of the ball. Nothing can happen until that very small, significant event occurs. It is not as easy as it looks, either. The first time a quarterback takes a snap from a center is actually a very awkward moment. When playing quarterback, the center bends over right in front of you. As quarterback, you are told to put your hands under the center, between his legs, and then push up so he knows that you are there. You are trying not to knock the center over, or hurt his ....um.... manhood, you are simply making it known that you are ready for the snap.

The relationship between a quarterback and a center is actually very intimate, when you think about it. These actions a quarterback does to and with a center are not something they would do with just anyone. If a man were to do this anywhere else in society, there would be a few raised eyebrows, don't you think?

I share that information because it was my ability to take a snap that allowed me as a freshman to make the travel squad to Norman, Oklahoma as the third quarterback. That was in 1981. I went along solely because I knew how to take a snap. That may be a little over-simplified, but it really did come down to the snap. Two of our top quarterbacks were injured. Another good player was redshirting and a redshirt freshman was having a hard time not fumbling snaps during practice. Thus, I was given the opportunity to suit up for my first varsity game.

I remember when Frank Solich, our freshman coach, found me walking to math class. I was surprised and found it just a little creepy that he could locate me among all the students on the large campus. He stopped his car and told me I would be practicing with the second-team offense during the week, and that I would be making the trip to Norman. What a crazy seven days that was. Only three months before, I had been fourth team on the freshman squad. Now, here I was taking snaps with the varsity.

Even though I was there with the group, I had no idea what was going on with the offensive plays. As you might recall, I had spent the last month running our opponent's plays on the scout team. Since I wasn't familiar with our offensive plays, I usually asked the other quarterback what I was supposed to do and tried not to look too stupid. For me, the most important thing was to NOT drop the ball when I took a snap. I didn't want to have to return to the "meat squad."

Bruce Mathison was the backup QB for this game. He was more than patient as he guided me through each practice. He tried not to laugh too hard when I mixed up the plays or threw to the wrong receiver. Nevertheless, I was living the dream. I had become a varsity quarterback for the fifth-ranked team in the country. During warm ups I was throwing passes to Todd Brown, Irving Fryer, Roger Craig, Anthony Steels, and a host of Husker legends. On one play, we ran an option drill and I made a pitch to future Heisman Trophy winner Mike Rozier. I wanted to stop and ask for an autograph.

Conversely, when I threw a bad pass, I would get "a look" from the receiver that seemed to ask, "What the %$^# are you doing out here?" I would apologize. What else could I do? One time, I accidentally called Roger Craig by Anthony Steel's nickname "Slick." Roger corrected me sharply saying, "MAN, don't you know who I am?" Clearly, I was out of place on the starting squad at that time.

I was out of place, but what an experience! I was traveling with the varsity. I felt like a rock star. When kids would come up to me for a signature, I would rebuff them and say, "Sorry kid. I'm nobody."

Before that game I was more nervous than I can recall ever being before or since. Warming up was emotionally traumatic as well. At Oklahoma's stadium, the grandstands are very close to the field. Some of the fans were yelling at us as we played catch to warm up. My heart was pounding so hard, I could barely get the ball out of my hands. I was shaking. Bruce just laughed at me. He knew I was having trouble with it all. I think the stress of that day is the origin of nightmares that I still have. Sometimes I still dream that I'm trying to throw a pass and the ball won't come out of my hand. Right now, I'm sweating just thinking about it.

But I never dropped a snap! At least, not until my junior year verses Oklahoma. That is a story for another time.

The Play: The Value of a Wife
"Enjoy life with your wife, whom you love, all the days of this meaningless life"
Ecclesiastes 9:9a

As I was searching for the best football analogy to describe the role that a wife plays in a man's life, I thought of many. A wife could be considered:

- **An Assistant Coach:** She helps with everything. She is engaged, involved, and ever-present. More importantly, she is there to give you the occasional kick in the pants when you need it!

- **A Running Back:** She does get a lot of hand-offs from the quarterback. Not only that, she quite often blocks for him. She handles the tasks of life effectively. She's a workhorse at times.

- **A Receiver:** I always want my wife to catch my passes (you know what I mean)! She must have great hands to juggle many tasks. She needs to be quick on her feet, able to dodge those pesky defenders.

- **A Coach Up in The Booth:** She does seem to have a bigger picture of what's going on. Her view is always unique. Her perspective is valuable. She provides insight and wisdom.

- **A Defensive Coordinator:** The best offense is a good defense. She seems to spot the obstacles that I struggle with more readily than I do. She loves to plan and to strategize.

I have to say that lineman, both offensive and defensive, are the most unselfish athletes on the team. They are the strong, dependable heroes of the game. They do all the dirty work and get very little credit for the success of the team. No offense is any good without a well-coordinated offensive line. A team can't win without scoring, and they can't score without a great line.

There is one position on the offensive line that directs everyone else, one player who makes most of the line calls and makes the whole thing work. Nothing happens until this guy says so. It's the center.

The center dictates where the huddle is and leads everyone to the line of scrimmage. Because of their dual leadership roles, the quarterback and the center have to been in sync all the time.

We are the family quarterbacks, and our wives are just like the center. We are designed to work in unison. We have to be together on the same page in the playbook to make life work. It is up to a husband as the family quarterback to coordinate with his wife, just as a quarterback coordinates with the center. We must understand her. When we do, she can have our back. This collaboration is our responsibility. It is up to us to make this connection productive.

The first scriptural insight that portrays this dynamic relationship is found in Genesis. The Lord God decided that it was not good for Adam to be alone, so He created a helper for him by taking a rib (ouch) and presenting to him "*woman.*" During that process, God gave us some guidance. *"For this reason a man will leave his father and mother and be united to his wife, and they will become one flesh."* 2:24. Within this proclamation we can gather some insight about why it is desirable for husbands and wives to be unified. Clearly, God knew what was best for man (men), and He knew what was to come. I say that because at this point there were no fathers or mothers!

God knew we would need to:

- **Leave our Fathers**

  Our dads are our spiritual authority, as well as our protectors and providers. When we get married, it is time for us to grow up and establish ourselves. I think this allows us to become reliant on Father God to be our authority. It is at this time that we can tap into the King of Kings for guidance, direction, and worthiness and begin to establish our own identity in Christ.

- **Leave our Mothers**

  Moms are typically our comforters. They fix our boo-boos, they show us affection, and they feel bad for us when life gets hard. If a man doesn't leave his mom's nurturing spirit when he gets married, it will drive a wedge between him and his wife. This is one of the major issues I have observed in couples that I work with.

  When a husband shows preference to his mother (and he usually doesn't realize that he is doing it) over his wife, this creates an emotional divide that is difficult for a husband and wife to overcome. If he looks to his mother for comfort, it usually means trouble.

- **Be United**

  Some translations use the word cleave, cling, or keep close. This concept describes a picture of separating from one entity (your mom and dad) and uniting with another (your wife). It is a very graphic illustration of how dramatic this change is. Learning to cleave to a wife is a necessary element for God's ultimate goal.

- **Be in Oneness**

  True oneness cannot happen without leaving mom and dad. We need to do so in order to build unity, develop a partnership, create an alliance, work together in collaboration, build a union, and live together in complete cooperation with our wife. At the same time, it can be painful and sometimes confusing when we are also told to *"honor your father and mother"* Ephesians 6:2. This becomes a tricky dance. We are charged with cleaving to our wife, while at the same time we are commanded to acknowledge and respect our parents.

The Stakes are High

Leading a family is a big responsibility. The consequences of how we do this can be lifelong. Scripture gives us a glimpse in 1 Peter 3:7: *"Husbands, in the same way be considerate as you live with your wives, and treat them with respect as the weaker partner and as heirs with you of the gracious gift of life, so nothing will hinder your prayers."*

- **Be Considerate**

  The word here actually means to have knowledge or understanding of. We are to understand our wives thoroughly. We are to understand their hearts, their minds and their emotions.

  "What?" you ask. "I need to understand her mind? Yes, and her emotions and how she thinks as well! Yes, you need to understand all of her!

  The principle I am describing here is a key to a successful marriage. Committing yourself to clearly understanding your wife is an essential part of building cooperation. If a man does not understand his wife, how can he draw conclusions about what she says or does? When learning how to get the snap of the ball from the center, I had to become familiar with the man as a part of the entire process. I need to understand my wife as well.

  In the overall scope of Husker football, players must embrace the idea that the multitudes are watching. Your personal reputation affects everyone who follows the team. In the same way, your reputation as a husband and family quarterback will suffer if you are not prepared to understand your wife.

- **Respect**

  We are to respect our wives. We need to respect their opinions, their thoughts and their perspectives. Many men wonder why their wives do not respect them. Perhaps it is because they as husbands are not sowing respect into the relationship.

  If a quarterback does not treat his center well, the center is likely to let him know by throwing a "look out" block. This happens when the center intentionally misses the defender and then he turns and shouts "look out!" just before the defender knocks the quarterback flat!

  I had a coach come up to me early in my career. He had heard that I tried to get into a bar one weekend while I was still underage. How he knew this scared me. He said, "You are a quarterback, you need to be above reproach." He challenged me to have respect for our team.

- **Weaker Vessel**

  This is where my analogy breaks down a little, however there are some similarities. If a quarterback disrespects his center, the quarterback is apt to get his @$$ kicked. Similarly, a wife will start to be disrespectful and do a little @$$ kicking of her own.

  A wife is not designed to handle the world in the same ways that you are. For example, she is not built to "support you." Many men want their wives to be "supportive." Well, why would the weaker vessel "support" the stronger one? That doesn't make sense does it? It's not her job. Many marriages break down this way.

  More is expected of quarterbacks on the team. In the same way, more is expected of a husband, the family quarterback. If you cannot accept this fact, you possibly need to rethink your position.

- **Heirs**

  We are bound in our inheritance of God's grace. We are His kids. Because we are children of the King of Kings, we should act like it.

- **Gift of Life**

  This life and the marriage that you are experiencing are a gift. They are a blessing and they reflect favor from God. Accordingly, a marriage should be treated with gratefulness and appreciation. We often take it for granted and don't treasure what has been given to us. The more we value all that God has provided, the more we protect and cherish it.

  Playing football for the University of Nebraska was something special. As players, we realized we were a part of something larger than ourselves. We valued it.

With our wives, it's the same. If we do not live with them in an understanding way, this scripture tells us we could face some dire consequences including hindered prayers. Wow. Really? If I don't understand my wife, respect her, value her partnership, and value this life, my prayers could be hindered? My relationship with God can be obstructed? Yes, they can.

Have you ever felt like your prayers were hitting the ceiling? Me too. Perhaps it's because our perspective needs to be adjusted. This can often be the consequence of not loving and esteeming our wives.

This was also true for those of us who disregarded the privilege of playing for Nebraska. If we wandered, we found ourselves on the bench or off the team. In the same way, how we value our wives will determine the course of our lives. Building unity will create trust and honor.

Reading the Defense
"This is now bone of my bones and flesh of my flesh"
Genesis 2:23a

There are many reasons why we men struggle with authentically understanding our spouses. I do not believe that any of us get married with the idea that we are going to treat our wives with indifference and hostility. The devil does a great job of leading us to that end just the same. He uses many of the things that I think are already hardwired into our inner man.

Training

I don't know about you, but I was not taught how to treat a woman in a way that made her feel respected and honored. That was NOT hardwired into me from the start. This is something I was expected to learn, somewhere along the way.

My father, whom I love deeply and who has passed away, didn't exactly teach me to be like Jesus to my wife. He didn't have very good training either. His father died when my dad was ten years old.

Dad had seven brothers and sisters, and he was raised by a widow who had quite the temper. Accordingly, he did not have a sound example of how to treat a wife in a way that Christ would, something that would have been demonstrated for him by his father. My father had no training, and so the training that I received from him was faulty. What most of us know about being a family quarterback is what we learned at home. Proverbs says that the glory of the child is his father. That is a serious consideration. It literally means that a child will watch his father and draw conclusions about who God is. There is *no greater responsibility than this*.

With that kind of example set before me in my own life, I learned that God must be angry, impatient, frustrated and intimidating. My father's example—my frame of reference—produced in me an unhealthy fear of the Lord. I did not see Jesus as someone you could come to when you were wounded. It took me many years of looking beyond my father to see Jesus with clarity.

Resolving Conflict

When it came to resolving conflict within a marriage, I was taught:

- If you get madder than she is, she will eventually shut up. I learned this while I was hiding under the kitchen table. I tried this early and often in my marriage. It worked but it didn't create the tenderness that I desired. What I didn't realize until I had already caused the damage was that no woman wants to have sex with a husband who is angry all the time.

- Her opinion is not as important as mine. Dad made this clear. I even used scripture to reinforce this terrible perspective in my marriage. Forgive me, Lord.

- She doesn't know what she is talking about. This is an excuse to dismiss her concerns. Carol's opinions were initially not valuable to me. This perspective ended up costing me a lot.

- She overreacts to everything. Carol's emotional responses were not validated and she eventually believed I hated her.

- If it gets too bad, threaten her. On many occasions, I was an abusive, arrogant and violent man.

Roles in the Home

When it came to roles of a wife in the home, I was taught:

- She cooks, and it had better be good.

- She cleans. I never saw my dad wash a dish.

- She needs to work. When I was growing up, my mom always had a job.

- The money is mine, or at least it is under my control. Most arguments between my parents were over finances.

I was totally unaware that I carried all of this baggage into our marriage. As Carol and I have worked with couples, we have discovered that most of us live our lives as seen through the lens that was created in the homes we grew up in.

Passive Fathers

I meet some men who were raised by passive fathers. These passive men taught their sons:

- Not dealing with conflict is actually a good way to deal with conflict.

- Mom just wants to control everything (and they are not going to let that happen to them).

- If you don't say anything, she will eventually shut up.

- If you ignore her long enough, she will go away, and when she does, it's her fault.

Viewing Her as a Possession

Another piece of unknown hard wiring that prevents real connection within a marriage, takes place at the wedding altar. I like to say that this is where we get altered.

It is at the wedding altar where two lives become one. This is a total change of scenery, spiritually. Unfortunately, for most of us, the wedding day is more like the culmination of a really big sales presentation we've made as a man, and the ceremony is the closing of our greatest sale ever. We won. She is ours.

Carol will tell you that on our honeymoon she felt "duped." She wondered what happened. She discovered that I felt like she belonged to me and she was now supposed to conduct life according to my wishes. It was as though she was no longer a human. In addition, when I used scripture to tell her why this was true, she was even more deceived. (See the chapter on understanding the playbook.)

This seems to be a common problem for men. We are hunters by nature. We go out and compete (hunt) for a degree. We compete to get a good job. When we find the woman of our dreams and make her our wife we have fulfilled the hunt. Now, it's on to the next goal. I hear wives tell me all the time that they feel like a possession and not an ally. If our enemy can get us to treat our wives like another conquest in life, he can put us at odds with them. He has won!

Fear of Emasculation:

During the years that Carol and I have traveled the country doing seminars, retreats, and counseling numerous couples, we have discovered that fear of emasculation is a common theme holding men back from becoming the sensitive warrior that God created them to be. Many men are being held hostage by a fear they hold in their own minds: they fear their own emotions.

Any time I bring up the idea that men should operate their lives from a perspective of emotional understanding and empathy, they often react by saying, "So, you want us to be like women?" This defensive response ultimately hinders a husband from gaining an understanding of his own emotions and the emotions of those under his care. Despite men's fears, this skill is required for success.

Our culture has placed a stigma on male *emotional intelligence* (understanding). Any man who can emotionally connect and identify with others is often considered effeminate. For some men, this is the greatest insult they could ever experience. So, how do we train men to become caring, thoughtful and engaging, if they are afraid for their manhood?

Is it possible that all these fears are a lie from the devil himself, whom scripture calls the father of lies? I believe they are. He lies to us, and too often we believe him.

From our perspective, this is one of the primary deceptions that the devil uses to keep men from accepting the help, input, and encouragement they need from their wives. Men sometimes believe that their wives want to control them, and that if they give up control, they are no longer men. When men operate with this perspective, they instantly become defensive regarding almost anything their wives say or do.

The enemy of your soul is going to work overtime to keep you from working on your relationship with your wife. If you truly understand, value and love her, YOU WILL BE A THREAT. Satan can't let this happen. The Lord God wants to sow good seed into your heart that will produce a harvest for generations. The devil will try to steal that for which Christ died. *"Resist him, standing firm in the faith, because you know that your brothers throughout the world are undergoing the same kind of sufferings."* 1 Peter 5:9

The Red Zone
"He who finds a wife finds what is good and receives favor from the Lord"
Proverbs 18:22

I wish I could tell you that I have always trusted Carol's insight. It took quite a while for me to discover the value, wisdom, and help that she provides. I will tell you this: Recognizing that she is my ally in life has been more precious than gold. *"Do not forsake wisdom, and she will protect you; love her and she will watch over you. Wisdom is supreme; therefore get wisdom. Though it cost all you have, get understanding."* Proverbs 4:6-7

Perhaps the greatest hurdle for a man in the process of living a united life with his spouse is seeing that his wife is on his side. Your wife is your teammate. She wants you to be significant. She is an asset not an adversary. She was created just for you. As we as husbands embrace that fact, we begin to prosper, thrive and experience life to the fullest.

Five Minutes Can Change Your Life

Over time I became more aware of Carol's tremendous discernment, so eventually I took advantage of her intuitions. I had built a bad reputation by coming home from work with a bad attitude, and in short order making a mess of things. My bad attitude could unravel the peace in our home very quickly.

It dawned on me one day that Carol was with the kids all the time, yet I thought that when I got home from work and had just entered the house, I knew what the kids needed. That was foolishness. So I made a deal with Carol. When I got home, she could tell me what needed to happen and I would follow through with it. Maybe I needed to check on Buddy or on Tiffani for some reason. Perhaps it was a night when I needed to help Carol with dinner. Whatever it was, I was committed. *"Submit to one another out of reverence for Christ."* Ephesians 5:21

Of course any time I would make those proclamations in an effort to become a better husband and father, I would face challenges to deter me from my objective. Just the same, I made that commitment and one day a challenge came my way. I never knew what the "tests," as I like to call them, would be. One particular evening a test came my way that would actually change my life forever.

At the end of the workday I pulled up in the driveway, just like every other day. During the day, I had talked to Carol a couple of times, (this was before cell phones) and nothing seemed unusual. Our children were young. Tiffani was five years old and Buddy was three. They were a handful, but nothing that Carol could not handle. I wasn't expecting a crisis, nor did I have any indication that a divine appointment was imminent.

As I came into the room where the children were playing, the thing that surprised me was Tiffani's attitude. She seemed particularly defiant and sassy to Carol. My first reaction was, "She needs to be disciplined. She cannot talk to you like that and get away with it." My sweet spouse replied, "No, she's had enough of that today. " She just needs some daddy time."

"I'll give her some daddy time," I growled, with a gesturing motion as if I were going to give her a spanking. Carol responded saying, "No, that's not what she needs."

I was thinking, "Is she nuts? This kid is treating Carol badly. Tiffani has a terrible attitude and she needs the spanking spoon!" I was at a crossroads. I had two choices: I could do the disciplinary thing and spank Tiffani (which I felt she needed), or, I could listen to my wife and heed her direction. I chose the latter! I said, "Okay, I can do that. If that's what you believe she needs, that is what I will do."

I went to Tiffani and asked her to sit with me. It was at this point that I set aside what I thought she needed and did what her mommy (my helper) thought she needed. "*There's a way that seems right to a man, but in the end it leads to death.*" Proverbs 14:12

Tiffani was reluctant, and continued to be very contentious. I prayed, "Lord, I really need you. Help me settle down. Help me meet the need of my little girl right now, in this moment." With a little more prompting, she was willing to sit on my lap. At first, she did not like it so she started squirming, and wrestling to get away. I resisted my inclination to scold her. I gently held her. I started whispering in her ear. "I'm sorry you've had a tough day. I know you are frustrated. Just sit with me for a while, it will be okay."

As I softly spoke to her, she settled down. The next thing I knew, she was curled up in my lap crying. I was shocked. I could hardly believe what was happening! She said she was sorry for having such a bad attitude. She was repentant and she became contrite. I don't think I could have produced a response like this by spanking her. She may have complied afterward, but her spirit wouldn't have demonstrated true remorse.

Wow! This "test" from God, took all of 5 minutes. I had acted like the quarterback that God had called me to be and Tiffani had responded by having a total change of heart. She quickly apologized to her mother.

As I share this experience with you, I still recall the feelings of that moment. They were and still are so intense. They still bring me to tears. I had experienced something special, something life giving. It was genuine. It was authentic and God-given. I had experienced true patience for the first time. It tasted very good.

More importantly, I had made a deliberate choice to listen to my wife and use the methods for caring for Tiffani that she recommended. It required me to reach out to the Lord in order to complete the challenge, but I was the one who received the most from it. I chose to receive the snap from Carol, and together we scored a touchdown!

Prayer

Lord, we love our kids. We need each other to pass along the mercy and grace that you have for us to share. Lead us to cooperate in an effort to demonstrate your love. We pray that our children will see you in us.
Amen.

Chapter 5
Get into the Game

In the last chapter, I told the story of the first time I suited up for a varsity game. I was able to make that trip to Oklahoma because of injuries to other players, but that didn't matter to me. I was thrilled to travel with the team. I got to stay at a nice hotel and, best of all, I got to receive the attention that comes with big-time football.

I had made it, I was in "the show"! I was even allowed to display the red "N" logo on my helmet, an honor you don't receive until you make it onto the Nebraska varsity football squad. Along with that, I was given football shoes and the coolest uniform anyone could possibly imagine. I don't even remember what number they gave me. While that was all very exciting, I was scared to death just the same.

As I said earlier, I was so nervous during warm ups I could barely get the ball out of my hand. The fans were so close to the field we could hear them screaming, making jokes, laughing, trying to get in our heads. It was so nerve wracking that I couldn't wait to get back to the safety of the locker room.

As we started to build an insurmountable lead over the Sooners, I began to get very nervous as I realized I might be asked to go into the game to take a few snaps. I was not ready for that and I hoped it wouldn't happen. Luckily it didn't. I didn't want to face the possibility of such a public embarrassment.

Once that traumatic episode had passed, it would be another two years before I finally got a chance to take a varsity snap. After a redshirt year, an ACL tear in the spring game and my first major knee operation, I was finally suited up and ready to go.

It was the fourth game of the 1983 season. That was the year that our team earned the nickname "The Scoring Explosion." Some of the more famous players on the team were Turner Gill, Irving Fryar and Mike Rozier. That year our prolific offense set several scoring records that still stand today.

After falling behind UCLA 10-0, we ran off forty-two straight points. Late in the fourth quarter, most of the backup players were put into the game and I got "the look" from Coach Osborne. I was excited. I thought my heart was going to jump out of my chest.

I went into the game and ran three or four plays, none of which I remember today. In those moments I finally fulfilled my dream. When I decided to attend the University of Nebraska it was with the hope of playing at least one play in Memorial Stadium in front of the most amazing fans in the world. I chose UNL over smaller schools, believing that one play there was worth more than four seasons anywhere else. I wasn't disappointed.

The incomparable high I was on that day served as a stark contrast to how I would feel my junior and senior seasons. I was no longer apprehensive to go into a game. After three years of preparation, I took the field with confidence week after week. I understood the offense in depth and in detail. I recognized different defensive sets. I knew exactly what I was required to do. I had done the preliminary work necessary to carry out my assignment. As a result, I had confidence in my preparation. I had trained diligently in the weight room. I spent time watching film. I practiced consistently. I was ready. Now it was up to me to make the most of the opportunities I was given.

I got my first start on October 13, 1984, against the Missouri Tigers. I didn't want to take that moment for granted. I realized that it might never happen again and I wanted to savor it. It was a cool fall afternoon. I recall looking around the stadium, seeing the faces of the fans and smelling the hot dogs cooking. I soaked in every moment. When my name was announced as the starting quarterback, I felt chills all over. I had dreamt about that moment since I was a little boy.

I must admit that I had a strange peace and calm. I was not nervous at all. All my preparation had equipped me for that day. It was as though I was walking into a moment that was created just for me and I knew it. It reminds me of Philippians 4:7. *"And the peace of God, which transcends all understanding, will guard your hearts and minds in Christ Jesus."* As the scripture says, the peace I felt made no sense. It transcended understanding.

The play I remember most from that game was a pass play that broke down. I had scrambled out of the pocket and headed up the field. When I turned toward the center of the field, there in front of me stood their middle linebacker. He was an imposing figure. I remembered having seen him on training films and recalled how intensely he was able to tackle his opponents. In this case, that would be *me*!

Acting instinctively, I ducked my head down to take him on. I knocked him backwards and he fell to the ground. He wasn't ready for me to run him over. The crowd went crazy. The fans rose to their feet and cheered loudly. That was the best feeling I would ever have on the football field. That day we beat the Tigers 33-23. During film session on Monday, we ran the play back repeatedly. One coach commented, "Travis, I think you cost him some cash in the draft."

What I lacked in physical ability I always tried to make up with sheer will. That perspective served me well as I started the next five games of the regular season. Not many walk-on quarterbacks get the opportunity that I had. I never wanted to waste the chance I was given.

The Play: Step onto the Field of Life
"In all these things we are more than conquerors through him who loved us."
Romans 8:37

Like the story I just shared with you, the game of life provides opportunities that we need to seize. These are moments given to us for success and learning. The playing field can be very intense. There are people watching. There are many players on that field for us to consider. The stakes are much higher in real life. The game of football has no eternal significance. However, our lives, the lives of our family and of those we influence have eternal significance.

The choices we make as the family quarterback will have an effect for generations to come. Numbers 14:18 tells us that *The Lord is long suffering, and of great mercy, forgiving iniquity and transgression and by no means clearing the guilty, visiting the iniquity of the fathers upon the children unto the third and fourth generation.* (KJV)

This is a very sobering scripture and it speaks directly to fathers. Its significance and the implications of what it means are important. Whether we realize it or not, we are playing this game for keeps. It's a battleground for the very lives of those under our influence.

A lot of men carry around lasting personal damage to their lives caused by ancestors. Is it possible that now is the time for that pain, destruction and dysfunction to stop? It can only end with us. More importantly, it can only end if we are aware of it and we recognize how it affects us. Only then will we be able to change the course of our lives in order to create a different heritage for our children and our children's children.

It is imperative that we as men of God get in the game with our families. Many men believe that going to work, paying the bills, coming home (most nights), doing the dishes occasionally and attending church weekly is "being in the game." I fear that we may have minimized the engagement that is required to lead our families.

Being in the game requires us to have a total commitment of mind, body and soul if we are to build a Godly heritage for our families. This is no small task. We should not attempt this with halfhearted reluctance. I think the time has come when our heavenly coach is giving us "the look" that means "get in there and show me what you've got!"

Dare to be Great

Theodore Roosevelt once said, "It is not the critic who counts; not the man who points out how the strong man stumbles, or where the doer of deeds could have done them better. The credit belongs to the man who is actually in the arena, whose face is marred by dust and sweat and blood; who strives valiantly; who errs, who comes short again and again, because there is no effort without error and shortcoming; but who does actually strive to do the deeds; who knows great enthusiasms, the great devotions; who spends himself in a worthy cause; who at the best knows in the end the triumph of high achievement, and who at the worst, if he fails, at least fails while daring greatly, so that his place shall never be with those cold and timid souls who neither know victory nor defeat." This is a passage from his famous speech, "Citizen in a Republic" presented in Paris in 1910.

Those words still ring true for dads as the family quarterback. Let us examine the mandates before us as men of God. God has granted us all the resources we need to accomplish His tasks. This kind of thinking will be our premise throughout this book.

The Bible is very clear about the roles and responsibilities of husbands and fathers. There are no expectations that seem to have a greater degree of accountability than these. The Apostle Paul does not hold back when he spells out the calling to men in Ephesians 5. In verses 1-2 he says, *"Be imitators of God, therefore, as dearly loved children and live a life of love, just as Christ loved us and gave himself up for us as a fragrant offering and sacrifice to God."* We are called by the Creator to model our lives after Jesus Christ. As part of that, we in return give ourselves as gifts to Him. We are to give our love to God and surrender to the will of the Father, just as Jesus did.

In Ephesians 5:3 Paul writes, *"But among you there must not be even a hint of sexual immorality, or any kind of impurity, or of greed, because these are improper for God's holy people."* If you need to, stop right here and get on your knees and repent for your current moral condition. Do it now. Let's start with a clean conscience.

If you are battling sexual sin, keep battling. Don't give in. Stay in the fight. This is where our enemy Satan wants to create a wedge between you and your spouse. If Satan gets into the bedroom, it's tough to get him out.

"Nor should there be obscenity, foolish talk or coarse joking, which are out of place, but rather thanksgiving." Ephesians 5:4. In the chapter of this book I call "Cadence" I cover the most powerful and dangerous instrument we possess: The words that come out of our mouths. We will see how taming our tongue is a challenging, demanding task. Learning how to talk with a heart of thankfulness is a lifelong task.

"For the husband is the head of the wife as Christ is the head of the church, his body of which he is the Savior." Ephesians 5:23. In keeping with our football analogies, I was always taught that wherever the head goes, the body follows. The same is true with husbands and wives. Wherever the husband leads, his wife will follow. These aren't my words; this is what the Bible says. What this verse is saying is clear. The questions we must ask ourselves are:

- What kind of leader am I?
- Do I inspire confidence?
- Do I create fear?
- Do I communicate well?
- Can my followers trust me?"

"Husbands love your wives as Christ loves the church and gave himself up for her." Ephesians 5:25. Wow! There is no other command in scripture quite like this one. Here we are told to be a living illustration of the Lord Jesus to another person. In the chapters that follow, we will look at practical applications of what it means to give yourself up for your wife.

When I have problems in my relationship with Carol, I always return to this verse and I ask myself, "Am I loving Carol like Christ loves me?" This requires me to allow God's love to affect me. Then, and only then, can I love her properly.

"...to make her holy, cleansing her by the washing with water through the word." Ephesians 5:26. What? It's up to *me* to make my wife holy? That is a dangerous premise to preach, let alone to try to live. This instruction suggests that I'm supposed to know God's Word so well that I can share it with my wife, and purify her in the process. That is why I need to know my playbook.

"...and present her to himself as a radiant church, without stain or wrinkle or any other blemish, but holy and blameless." Ephesians 5:27. Wait a second! I present my wife to Christ as clean, and pure, and she gets no blame? Okay, I know that's a lot to take in. Don't get mad at me. I didn't write it. I'm just attempting to discover what it means in my own life. I'm trying to live this out. If it is in the Word, I know it to be true. Each time I read it, I'm convicted.

This verse reminds me of the dream I had where I saw Carol's burnt and disfigured spirit. Whether we realize it or not, we bring our wives to Christ in the condition that we have created. That is why we are to love our wives like Christ loves us! There is no getting around it. This will be our yardstick for evaluating our conduct as the family quarterback.

There is the good news: He will equip us, train us and walk with us. There is a greater reward for those of us who are willing to get into the game: *heaven right here on earth.* That is exactly what Jesus taught us when he prayed to his father, *"Your kingdom come, your will be done on earth as it is in heaven."* Matthew 6:10. That's precisely what I want. I want my own little slice of heaven, right here, right now! I'm enjoying mine and you can enjoy yours, too.

Reading the Defense
"The accuser of our brothers, who accuses them day and night."
Revelation 12:10b

Some personality types engage in life more readily than others. Some men are more willing to walk into the fire. Others walk away from the fire, while still others will stand and watch the fire burn. No matter what a man's natural disposition might be, we all need to become acutely aware of the position and power that we possess as the family quarterback. We need to step up and get into the game! I think the enemy of our souls has created obstacles that keep men from wholeheartedly getting in the game, don't you? These obstacles include fear and shame.

Fear

Just like that game in Norman, Oklahoma, my freshman year, fear can grip us like a vise. It can have a totally paralyzing effect on our minds, our bodies and our spirits. Fear can keep us from engaging with our families when conflicts occur. It can prevent us from getting involved in our children's education, with their activities and in disciplining them if they need it.

Fear might even distract us from developing an intimate relationship with the Lord Jesus Christ. The question I have to ask myself when I experience fear is this: "What am I really afraid of?" If I'm able to gain some understanding of the things that cripple me, I can begin to overcome those fears. I can name several types of fears that I have wrestled with:

- **Losing and Failure**

  I hate losing. I am a poor loser. I don't handle setbacks well. I don't like playing games that I'm not good at.

  Because the way I live tends to be performance-based, I see life as a pass/fail experience. If things don't go well, I instantly feel like I am a failure. If I need to engage members of my family, I risk failing. When obstacles occur, will I take those opportunities to learn or will I retreat? The devil wants us to back off. The way we view these challenges is determined by our willingness to face them.

- **Conflict**

Disagreement can be terrifying to my soul. I can get sick to my stomach when I am involved in conflict. Frequently I experience conflict when I am forced to make a difficult choice. At times like this I need to press on despite the alternative of taking a seat on the bench.

Conflict causes me to fear the disappointment I may cause someone else and how they will feel about me. I am a people pleaser to the core. Being concerned with how people feel about me reveals just how much that controls me. It is easier for me to concede than it is for me to lead.

When we choose not to engage we grow bitter. Not surprisingly, that is just what the devil wants. Each day brings with it more conflicts. What we need to realize is that God gives us the ability to face conflict. Whether we decide to do that or not is up to us.

- **Past Setbacks**

Satan loves to throw our failures in our faces. He uses every mistake we have ever made to keep us on our heels. I can be so wrapped up in the fear of my past haunting me that I don't think I'm qualified to lead. The same holds true for you.

Satan will take your fumbles and interceptions and make you feel unworthy of your position. He wants you to run to the locker room where you think it's safe. Just because I have thrown my share of interceptions doesn't disqualify me from being a successful quarterback.

- **Passive Nature**

Some men by their very nature are more passive and reserved than others. These men are often competent, articulate, and very successful in their work. They may be well-respected by their peers. At home, however, they are inactive, lethargic and withdrawn. It's as though all the confidence they exhibit outside the confines of their family environment evaporates once they encounter those who count on them the most.

These passive men also operate with the same fear I described earlier, but their fear is multiplied exponentially. These men can be characterized as those who view the glass as half full. They operate in a frame of mind that always sees a worst-case scenario. This causes them to freeze in almost every conflict.

They are slow to react to circumstances because they think through their responses very carefully. Their silence or hesitation is often misunderstood as apathy. Because these men tend to be reserved emotionally, they come across as being under control, kind, and thoughtful. Their wives, on the other hand, know that is not the case. The wife of one of these men may become increasingly agitated by her husband's passivity. Her reaction may cause him to retreat even further, making her even more aggravated.

Passive men operate by avoiding conflict at all costs. This is contrary to a quality leadership perspective. This story line is playing out every day in Christian homes. The family quarterback is sitting on the bench paralyzed while his center is in the middle of the field screaming at him.

Shame

The greatest weapon that the devil possesses is shame. Most often, it is the shame of sin. He will drive you into isolation by using your humanity against you.

It all started in the Garden of Eden. That was the most perfect stadium ever created. Satan took the innocence of Eve and the disobedience of Adam and together they introduced "the calamity of turnovers." The result of their actions caused a condition that we are still trying to overcome today. In shame they hid from God. Along with that they forfeited the life that God had planned for them. Shame has been plaguing us ever since.

Shame is a force that drags us into darkness. It makes us believe that this deep barren desolate place in our hearts is a place that has no redemption. Shame tells us there is no hope, grace or mercy for us in that place. This is Satan's dungeon. He wants to lead us into it and imprison us there.

To the family quarterback it is worse than being fourth team on the depth chart. The sad fact is that men by nature gravitate toward this prison consistently. *"Men loved darkness instead of light because their deeds were evil."* John 3:19b

The devil uses our sin to convince us that we are not deserving of love. If we don't believe we are worthy of being loved, we are incapable of receiving the love of our wives and even worse, the love of God.

Shame can cripple the family quarterback by:

- Creating disconnection. No uniform for you. You're not worth being on the team.

- Crushing dreams. No bowl game either. You are a loser.

- Causing you to judge others. You are critical of your teammates.

- Forcing you to lash out to inflict pain in others. Fighting with your teammates.

- Isolating you. You hide in the locker room.

- Making you believe you are not good enough. Why bother studying the playbook?

- Relentlessly accusing you. This is like having a coach that you can never please.

"I have come into the world as a light, so that no one who believes in me should stay in darkness" John 12:46. Shame is the misbelief that you are what you do. Since you are a sinner, you are a failure, so you should be ashamed. If Satan can get us to focus on our sin then we aren't free to come into the light. If we don't come into the light, we will not be able to experience the grace and mercy that Jesus bought for us upon the cross. The devil is determined to keep us on the bench, which unfortunately is where we bring our family as well.

The Red Zone
"Courage is not the absence of fear, but rather the assessment that something else is more important than fear."
Franklin D. Roosevelt

Some husbands just don't think they are ready to go onto the field, much like I was my freshman year. Yet, as God's family quarterback, we are already on the field, especially here in the Red Zone! We need to take a cue from John Wayne who said, "Courage is being scared to death, but saddling up anyway." It's time to put on our helmets, jerseys and cleats, because the game is happening and our team is waiting.

If I were to document the number of mistakes I have made in my twenty-eight years of marriage it would take volumes. What I am learning is that each mistake I make has a lesson attached to it. As a part of Jesus' redemption for us, He wants us to learn and become more educated. Quarterback school is always in session.

It is up to us to "*be careful, then, how you live--not as unwise but as wise, making the most of every opportunity, because the days are evil.*" Ephesians 5:15

It is our obligation to allow the Holy Spirit to help us sort through each of our experiences. Gaining wisdom comes as we surrender. I quoted this scripture from Ephesians on the day I learned of my season-ending knee surgery during my senior year. This verse helped me on that troubling day.

I experienced one of those opportunities to live as someone wise one Sunday morning when the kids were little. Tiffani was four and Buddy was two. We had made a habit of attending church. As usual, we were running late. When I had gotten myself ready, I went out to the van to wait for Carol and the kids. I sat there patiently. (At least I thought I was patient.) This was our regular routine. I got ready to go and they were lagging behind.

I hate being late for anything, especially for church. It's embarrassing to come in after worship has started, then to squeeze into a pew and make everyone else uncomfortable. This is so unnerving for me. I really get frustrated with being late for church. (Can you hear how my main concern is the shame that this causes me? Can you feel my frustration?)

I was getting ready to hit the horn (because I know that will help them, right?). Fortunately, I had a moment of clarity. I thought, "I wonder if she needs some help?" I know how pathetic that sounds, yet that is exactly what happened.

I went inside. Carol was in our bathroom getting herself ready. I stood in the doorway for a second and I decided *not* to say something snarky like, "Still working on the war paint?" Instead, I asked her, "How can I help?"

She looked at me a little puzzled. She was wondering if my inquiry was sincere. She was apprehensive because we had had this discussion before and it had never ended well. I had a tendency to get upset, which made our trip to church very uncomfortable.

In an attempt to give me some insight, she asked me, "Who did you get ready this morning?" It was a rhetorical question, but it had a tremendous impact. I sheepishly looked at myself in the mirror and said, "Me! I did pretty good, huh?"

That wasn't a very good answer. It didn't take long for me to re-think her question. Finally, I understood her point. Meanwhile, she began making a list of ways that I might be more helpful on Sunday mornings.

"I could use your help," she began. Then she started a list so extensive that I was floored. There were at least ten things she needed to accomplish on days before she would be able to leave the house. As I listened it dawned on me that I could do all of them. I know what you are thinking, and yes, I was that unaware of how *un*helpful I really was to Carol.

I had not pitched in to get the kids dressed, get the pets fed, get everyone some breakfast, etc. At that moment, it occurred to me that in fact **I wasn't in the game! I was a spectator!** I expected Carol to handle these chores while I waited in the van for her to show up. I vowed in my heart that morning to engage and participate more effectively. I vowed to get into the game!

This experience helped me realize the massive number of responsibilities that Carol handled all the time. I had a new gratefulness and appreciation for her. It made me start to wonder what else was going on in our world that I was missing. I quickly realized the list of things I was missing could be very extensive.

Now that time has passed I must tell you that getting into the game has been the most gratifying endeavor of my life. Engaging in family life has created a new practical application for God's Word. It also has helped me to become more qualified to give my input and to be able to offer an opinion when it is requested. By getting into the game in this new way, I was fulfilling Psalm 37:3. *"Trust in the Lord and do good; dwell in the land and enjoy safe pasture."* This verse demonstrates how the family quarterback can't make a difference until he gets off the bench and goes out onto the field. He has to have the courage to put his helmet on, talk to the coach, get the play and run onto the field.

Prayer

Dear Lord, give me courage to engage my family. Help me to see the authority and power to lead that you have granted me. Give me strength and wisdom as I get into the game of life. Amen.

CHAPTER 6
THE HUDDLE

I have to laugh. I say that because using the analogy of "The Huddle" is really not appropriate in today's football scene, since teams really don't huddle up much anymore. The huddle is becoming obsolete in football, but we can still use it to make a point.

Because teammates spend so much time together, just like when they are in the huddle, they develop a very strong bond. In my case, thirty years later I am still in touch with many of the guys I competed with.

In my days of playing football, the huddle served as the most critical point of communication for a team during the game. Nothing happened until we gathered, shared the strategy and called the play. The center decided where the huddle would take place. He put his arms up and yelled, "huddle" to signal for everyone to gather around him. The coach would send in the play to the quarterback via one of the players, usually a receiver. Then the QB would tell the team the call and give them the snap count. Everyone would clap their hands when the QB said "break." The team would then go to the line and execute the play. That was the old school style of play calling.

Now coaches signal the plays with gestures and billboards. It's almost comical watching the sidelines with all the motions and banners. This transfer of information is critical. If one aspect of the play is misinterpreted, it can lead to real problems. In earlier days, the humorous part of our system was when the receivers gave the plays to the quarterback. Some of our play calls were rather lengthy. Occasionally the message would be scrambled by the time it got to me. It was my job to make sense of whatever I was told. One time I received the message: "I right, fake, flat." So I called: "I right, forty-six, iso pass, two delay flat." That was what the call was actually named. As you can see, I needed to be able to anticipate what plays the coaches might be expected to call in the current situation and then translate what I was told into what would become the correct call.

The huddle was not the only time we would meet as a team. In fact I was shocked at the number of meetings we had throughout the season. We would actually spend more time in meetings than we would on the practice field. Every day the quarterbacks met with Coach Osborne. We would review any new plays we were installing and analyze the defense we were going to face in the upcoming game. Coach was a meticulous tactician who would methodically break down the strategies of our opponents. After these "position meetings," the whole offense would gather together. We would review the film from the previous day's practice and go over any adjustments we needed to make.

Each week we had a scouting report for the upcoming opponent. We studied their formations, their tendencies and their personnel. We set goals for rushing yardage, passing yardage, points and most critically, our turnovers (that goal was always zero). Each Monday we would use those goals as our reference for how well we performed the previous weekend. Coach instilled in us the belief that if we performed to our ability, winning would take care of itself. We were actually competing against ourselves and how perfectly we executed our plans.

On game day the meetings continued. We started with chapel, where Coach would have a pastor or former player share his faith with us to encourage us as part of our motivation. After breakfast we got together for more film review of our opponent to confirm our strategies. At the stadium, Coach would give us the warm up schedule. Some positions would meet with their respective coaches for final instructions. The coolest part was right before the entire team took the field. One or two of the captains would give a little speech. I'll never forget the time Turner Gill told us, "That's two down. Let's go get number three." Each week during the 1983 season he did the same thing, updating the numbers of games won. He did that all the way to our undefeated 12-0 regular season. After the captain's talk, Coach Osborne would come in and we all would kneel for prayer.

Coach was not a "rah, rah" kind of guy. He didn't raise his voice or get too excited. He would remind us of our preparation, our superior conditioning and our talent. He would often tell us that by the second half our three-yard runs would turn into six-yard runs and our six-yard runs would turn into ten-yard runs, etc. His faith in the system and the strategy was contagious.

During the game offensive and defensive units would meet on the sideline between each series. Coaches would use a chalkboard to draw diagrams and to make adjustments throughout the game. The assistant coaches would chart the defensive alignments and Coach would review those with the quarterbacks. He was always open to what we were seeing on the field. He even would ask what we thought about certain plays. It made players feel like they were a part of the process.

At halftime we got together again. The coaches would use their chalkboards to highlight all the defenses we had seen so far. They would list the plays they thought would be successful. The coaches would ask the linemen what they were seeing in regards to stunts and blitzes. It was a group effort. Everyone had a part. Everyone had a unique view of the game. Each man's perspective was valued and integrated into the overall plan.

After the game, Coach would give us a brief review of his thoughts. He was always positive and he always offered some encouragement, especially on things we needed to work on. Even though our goal was perfection in our execution, he never belittled us for failing in our objectives. His mind was always on the next opponent, our preparation and the bigger picture.

The Play: Connect and Communicate with Clarity

"Let us not give up meeting together, as some are in the habit of doing, but let us encourage one another."
Hebrews 10:25a

Do you remember when you were dating your spouse? If you were like most of us, you spent a lot of time together. I remember hours and hours of sitting and just talking with Carol. I tried to spend as much time as I possibly could with her. I would go way out of my way just to be with her. If we weren't together, we were talking on the phone. I never got tired of it.

A funny thing happens after the wedding ceremony. We seem to move on to other priorities. It's pretty typical to start disconnecting from our wives right after we get married. This sad reality must be approached with deliberate intention if anything in the relationship is going to change.

When Carol and I moved to Phoenix in 1987 we started attending a couples' Bible study called The Christ Quest Institute. It is a three-year discipleship program to help husbands to love their wives like Christ would. This was a life-changing endeavor that helped us establish habits that would become foundations in our marriage.

Thirty-Minute Huddles

The first project assignment was "give your wife thirty minutes of undivided attention every day." This seemed like a reasonable consideration until we attempted to do it. We quickly discovered it wasn't as easy as we had thought. With Carol and me, these half hours regularly turned into a time for arguments instead of my listening to her.

I had to learn to listen to Carol. I was great at talking, but not very astute at listening. More incredibly, I was even less skilled at *hearing*! This process helped me to discover the deep anger in my heart that I had to deal with. It was like James 1:19 was written just for me. *"My dear brothers, take note of this: Everyone should be quick to listen, slow to speak and slow to anger, for man's anger does not bring about the righteous life that God desires."*

Spending time listening to Carol was much like being in the huddle as a player. Listening takes intentional discipline. It must be approached with consistent determination, or it won't happen.

In the same way as the team gathers for the huddle, huddles between Carol and me have become a cornerstone for our lives to this day. If we are ever feeling disconnected from one another, the first thing I do is huddle with her. We need that.

Our willingness to spend one-on-one time with our wives is the best gift we can give them. It enhances our ability to lead the family. It creates the necessary cooperation, communication and insight to get the job done. Without huddling there is no way that we can truly understand what our family is experiencing or what they need. To be effective, we need insight from all our teammates. How can we possibly call the next play if we don't huddle?

There are a few things I must consider as I conduct these huddles:

- **Unity**

  We are a team. This is not a dictatorship. Everyone has a perspective about the game and how they are being affected in it. We need to create an environment where the members of our team feel valued by us. We must look them in the eye and listen to their perspectives. This will help to create unity.

  My attitude toward Carol will determine whether or not she feels like an indispensable part of my life. As Coach Osborne was known to respect the opinions and views of all his players, we, too, must allow our family to have input. *"Make every effort to keep the unity of the Spirit through the bond of peace."* Ephesians 4:3. This activity can even take place at the dinner table if we make it a priority. Taking the time to gather as a family allows all the members of our team to feel they are valuable.

- **Loyalty**

  Do my family members know that I have their backs? Do they feel like they are a priority in my world? Or do they feel attacked and criticized?

  Football teams establish a culture of allegiance by making every member of the team feel special. In a family this is critical as well. Does your star student get priority in the family? Does your struggling child feel less worthy of your attention? Most importantly, does your wife know beyond any doubt that you are in her corner? This is established through listening and receiving her point of view.

- **Humility**

  If I approach these family huddles with the posture of superiority I will not create a healthy exchange of perspectives. It is important for me to set aside any predetermined conclusions about the circumstances or subjects we are addressing. I must be willing to set aside my need to be right. There is value in opening ourselves up to new understanding. Matthew 23:12b gives us a glimpse of the benefits of humility, *"whoever humbles himself will be exalted."* When

I forced my opinion on *my* team, our huddles would often get side tracked. These exchanges would lead to everyone feeling frustrated and disregarded. I needed to return to the principles of listening.

- **Consistency**
Consistency is a hallmark of all great leaders. If you are going to set the standard of meeting with your spouse and your kids, it needs to be regular. My daily meetings with Carol were a non-negotiable part of our lives. That habit then turned into weekly meetings with the kids for reading, planning and dreaming. We protected our meal times and our Sunday evenings to make sure we were together during those times. In an effort to create consistency our motto was "I go, you go, we go." We were living life together and the kids knew it.

  Every January Carol and I still meet to look over the previous year's calendar and reminisce about the provisions of God and the many people and adventures we have experienced. Psalm 1:3 describes what a consistent husband looks like: *"He is a tree planted by streams of water, which yields its fruit in season and whose leaf does not wither, whatever he does prosper."* Our consistency grows as the roots of our commitment become deep and unwavering.

- **Accentuate the Positive**
There is an old saying that you can catch more flies with honey than you can with vinegar. This same principle works in our homes. One of my main objectives in our meetings with families is to help them take the lemons of life and turn them into lemonade. For example when we are having dinner with others, we go around the table and ask each person to share their "blessings and bummers" of the day.

  This time of sharing gives everyone an opportunity to express the things that encouraged them and at the same time acknowledge the painful aspects of life. It also offers an opening for us to see if we believe that *"in all things God works for the good of those who love him, who have been called according to his purpose."* Romans 8:28. What we have found over time is that life brings us lessons from which to learn, and in those lessons we can find value. The only way we can teach these lessons to our children is by living them out ourselves.

- **Prepare to Learn**

    Coach Osborne often went around the room to check on the players to see how they were doing. He wanted to know what things were working for them and what aspects of the game they found difficult. In this way, we all were able to gain insights into our teammates. We all needed to inquire, listen and learn. Using this technique also helped me to become more proficient in the art of asking good questions. In this way I was able to learn more about the hearts and minds of my teammates.

    I have heard that the best listeners use the 80/20 rule. They talk only 20 percent of the time while they listen the other 80 percent. I can learn to be a good listener if I'm willing to be daring. For example, I can tell my wife that this is my goal. When she is aware of that, she can help me!

    Just be warned; your wife may actually assist you with this commitment to leadership. How well you do with this experiment will reveal if you have a teachable spirit. Can you listen to her input? Are you able to allow her insight to strengthen your ability to lead effectively? Similarly, this will give you a chance to model a learner's spirit in front of your children. That allows us to follow the sensible advice of Solomon in Proverbs 10:19. *"When words are many, sin is not absent, but he who holds his tongue is wise."*

- **Give Feedback**

    Communication is a very tricky business. How many times have you thought you were on the same page with your wife or kids, only to find out that you had totally different understanding about what was said during a conversation? This still happens all the time to me.

    Clarification becomes vital to our discussions. The "feedback technique" is often helpful. This is simply the habit of feeding back to the other person what we heard them say. For instance, I might respond to Carol's statement with: "What I hear you saying is..." This gives her a chance to clarify or confirm what she said.

Just like in a football huddle, I as the quarterback, or in this case as the spiritual leader of the family, need to decipher the content of the message and discern its actual meaning. Using techniques like this, I make it my responsibility to be an accurate communicator. As on the playing field, I don't want to be running the wrong play in life!

It is up to us to understand our wives and children. If we commit to communicating with clarity and consistency, we will be like *"the one who received the seed that fell on good soil is the man who has the word and understands it. He produces a crop, yielding a hundred sixty or thirty times what was sown."* Matthew 13:23

"On two, on two, ready, break!"

Reading the Defense

"I tell you that if two of you on earth agree about anything you ask for, it will be done for you by my Father in heaven. For where two or three come together in my name, there am I with them."
Matthew 18:19-20

The devil is very familiar with Jesus' words in Matthew 18. He knows that keeping believers at a distance from one another gives him the advantage. He knows that is especially true when it comes to husbands and wives. He seems to have found that an excellent way to bring down the power of Christianity is to separate husbands and wives, especially if they have children. Once he has the mom and dad at odds, the devil comes in and deceives the children.

It doesn't take much effort to look around our world and see that this strategy is working. How many divorced couples with children do you know? Can you see the pain and confusion in the kids? The Barna Group reports that 60 percent of kids raised in Christian homes are not returning to church as adults. Satan's scheme for keeping the saints from huddling is working famously. His strategy is also multi-faceted.

Life Happens

The disconnection with our families does not occur over night. It's like the frog that is immersed in a pan of cold water and ultimately becomes cooked as the water temperature is increased to boiling. You turn the heat on and the frog doesn't even know it's being cooked. Before too long, the frog is lunch. I know you don't eat frog, but you get the picture. Satan sees us as frogs in a pot of water, and he wants to kill us by turning up the heat.

The busyness of the world can suck us in. Even things that seem good for us can create disconnection. When Carol and I moved to Phoenix to be in full-time ministry, I was expected to be at church Sunday morning, Sunday night and Wednesday night. This was not healthy for a young family like ours. While I'm a full-fledged proponent of church, I've learned that it's better to practice godliness at home than attend another church service.

When our children begin to get older, they start having a never-ending list of activities. Have you seen a little league baseball schedule? It's incredible. It's not a bad thing to allow your little ones to compete or participate in a multitude of activities. If you are not diligent about time management, however, it can end up controlling your schedule.

Life can be exhausting when you try to do it all. When you are busy with activities, time devoted to family huddles may suffer. If we don't protect our time together, it will evaporate.

Pursuit of Happiness

Within the heart of every man is a certain amount of discontentment. We all possess a yearning for more of something that seems like it can never be fulfilled. For most of us, it's that God-shaped hole that only Jesus can fill. It's in this void that the devil can attach his secret hook. He knows that discontent is a major weakness in our lives and he routinely uses it to entice us. Not surprisingly, he uses a variety of different baits to hook us:

- **Validation**
  We all want to feel successful. We all need to be validated. If the devil can get us to turn our eyes away from Jesus to fulfill our desire for significance, he wins. He can lure us into a multitude of endeavors that separate us from faith and family. For example, climbing the corporate ladder seems like a valid dream, filled with opportunities that seem legitimate.

Advancement in our jobs frequently involves meeting even greater expectations. Working more hours and traveling more often separate us from our families. It seems like the better the job title, the less we are at home. Suddenly, we find we are fulfilling Ecclesiastes 2:22-23: *"What does a man get for all the toil and anxious striving with which he labors under the sun? All his days his work is pain and grief; even at night his mind does not rest."*

I have spent many restless nights creating new business dreams and objectives. My human nature is never fulfilled. There is always more to accomplish. This too is meaningless.

- **Provision**

Most Christian men will tell you that they work hard to provide for their families. The reality, however, often is that they have buried themselves in so much debt they have to work all the time just to keep what they have.

I have had many wives tell me they would prefer to live a more modest life if it would mean that their husbands would actually be home more. Sadly, we often find that if he's going to spend his life *making* money, she may be more willing to *spend* it...*ALL!* This too is meaningless.

How much is enough? That is the real question. Where is the satisfaction?

After Carol and I were married and I graduated from college, we needed another vehicle. For weeks I had visited a local motorcycle dealership where I drooled over a Midnight Black Yamaha Virago 750. Eventually, I bought one.

The first day I had my new prized possession, I tipped it over and broke the mirror. I think the Lord was telling me, "You love that bike a little too much." *"Whoever loves money never has money enough; whoever loves wealth is never satisfied with his income. This too is meaningless."* Ecclesiastes 5:10.

I remember when earning $2,000 per month was awesome. I did and I spent it. As that number grew, I still spent it. That kind of lifestyle is a financial trap that is the perfect distraction to keep us from huddling.

- **Pleasure**
  What is your chosen pleasure? What is it that you can't wait to do? What do you lie awake at night thinking about? Golf? Tennis? Horses? Cars? ATVs? Gambling? Fiction? Movies? News? Sports? Businesses? Hunting? Biking? Fitness? Cards? Speed? Risk? Adrenaline? Okay, I'll say it: for most men, the answer is *sex*. None of these is inherently wrong or sinful. They all, however, can distract you from becoming the family quarterback you were meant to be, especially sex.

  The most insidious of these pleasures for a married man is a hidden sexual life. Nothing will cripple your world more than allowing yourself to be sexually gratified by someone other than your wife. *"All things are wearisome, more than one can say. The eye never has enough of seeing, nor the ear it's fill of hearing."* Ecclesiastes 1:9. Who has time to huddle with all that fun? We can spend our lives creating a wealth of toys and belongings, only to lose it all in the end. *"What good is it for a man to gain the whole world, yet forfeit his soul?"* Mark 8:36. This too is meaningless.

- **Isolation**
  The result of sin in the Garden of Eden was separation of Adam and Eve from God. That is exactly what Satan knew would happen and his plan worked. He wants to get you alone. He wants to separate you from your family by any means possible.

  While Satan is tempting us with all the things of the world to get us distracted, he is also going to use various tactics to entangle our hearts and isolate us.

- **Relational Inadequacies**
  Satan wants us to believe that we can't lead, discipline or influence our family. Because we men tend to be inadequate in relationship discussions, we often are more likely to work on the car than talk to our wives. That is right up Satan's alley. I know men who work long hours at least in part because they are lost at home talking to their wives. A loss of confidence is another way of keeping us from huddling.

- **Independence**

  The nature of men is fiercely driven by a need for independence. That's why we can't wait to leave home. We don't want to "need" anyone. We desire to make our own way. Do you think God knew something when he said, *"it is not good for man to be alone"?* Genesis 2:18a. Who can huddle when he is alone?

- **Guilt**

  Deep in the heart of Christian men is a strong longing to lead well. Unfortunately, most of us have created a great deal of damage along the way. The devil hammers away at us using our failures to belittle us. Because we don't want to cause more damage and again be a failure, it often seems easier to do nothing than to engage and make another mess. It's like allowing a turnover in football. Turnovers keep us from huddling.

- **Resentment**

  This is the poison that fueled my own anger and repeatedly drove me into solitude. The hardness of my heart due to unresolved conflicts built up and prevented me from seeing clearly. Even if I was correct in my discussions with Carol, my bitterness created an unrighteousness that disqualified my leadership.

In my twenty years of working with men and helping them improve their relationships, this is the most significant cause of disconnection. No one wants to huddle with an angry quarterback. Keeping us from huddling disables our offense. This keeps the team from functioning with the efficiency that it was designed for. We can have a great game plan, but if we don't huddle it won't work.

The Red Zone

"'For I know the plans I have for you,' declares the Lord, 'plans to prosper you and not harm you, plans to give you hope and a future.'"
Jeremiah 29:11

The hope for a prosperous life looked pretty dim after Carol left me. It was more than a month before she moved back home. She returned on the condition that I move out for a while. Life looked pretty grim. I was ashamed and embarrassed because I was in full-time ministry and I couldn't even keep my family together. I went to my boss to let him know that I had to step back and re-evaluate my life and my faith. He told me, "take your time, you can use your desk here to get things figured out." Two weeks later as I was hunting for my next job opportunity he told me, "I have someone for your desk."

Things seemed even bleaker. I was out of a job. At the same time, however, the Lord was working on my heart. Within a few weeks my attitude began to change and Carol could see that. After talking about how we could rebuild our relationship, she let me come back home and the process started.

I began substitute teaching during the day. It was interesting being in junior and senior high schools all over the city. I found the metal detectors in the downtown schools to be a little unnerving. I learned that I wasn't in Nebraska anymore, Toto. Unfortunately, the income from part-time teaching was not adequate to meet our monthly budget. I needed a second job to help make ends meet.

Domino's Daddy Delivers

I recalled a friend of mine who had been down on his luck and who went to work for Domino's Pizza as a delivery driver. Carol reminded me of this and I thought, "Man, I'm no pizza guy." Instead, I found a security guard opening. I thought at the time, "That's pretty cool, they've got uni's (uniforms)."

After a short training period with the security people, I was a teacher by day and security guard by night. I was a little like a super hero, right? My first assignment was an all-nighter looking after an open electrical transformer cabinet. That should be easy for a super hero, shouldn't it? It got chilly outside, so I jumped in my truck to warm up. I quickly fell asleep. A supervisor banging his flashlight on my window interrupted my deep REM sleep. My next call was to Domino's.

Things really started to turn around for Carol and me. To my surprise, my willingness to do whatever it took to provide for the family, even if it meant delivering pizza, blessed her! She started to feel like she was important to me.

I stayed focused on our regular huddles. My purpose changed from winning arguments with Carol to really getting to know her. I began appreciating her for who God made her to be. I really fell in love with her all over again. We began to experience joy together for the first time.

Carol would bring the kids by the pizza store just to say hi. I would put Tiffani up on the counter and feed her pepperoni. I was working two jobs and our lives became more connected. I took every free moment to spend time with my family. All other things in my life diminished and we started to thrive as a family. They would sing to me when I left in the evenings "Domino's Daddy Delivers."

I was the closing driver one night. I had to clean up everything to help close the store. I was washing dishes in back room. I started to reflect on my life and how things in it were getting better.

So many people thought I had "backslidden in my faith." Just a few months ago, I had traveled the country as a Husker and an evangelist. To onlookers I was now a failure, delivering pizza.

Yet, for the first time in my life I had authentic peace. It was the peace that scripture says *"passes understanding."* When I began to realize how good God was, I wept uncontrollably as I washed those dishes. I'm pretty sure my coworkers thought I was crazy.

Because I was a reliable hard worker, I started to gain favor with the manager. He would give me the busiest time slots and he would give me time off when I asked for it. Every night he allowed me to make a special pizza to take home. Carol loved that benefit.

Two jobs were not enough to pay the mortgage, however, and we fell into default. I did not want to lose the house. We had made the down payment with a small inheritance we received when Carol's dad died. I was not about to let that go.

What would it take to put you in this car?

So I did the natural thing. I got into the car business. I hear you laughing. That was supposed to be my career path because my dad was a car dealer. I grew up in the business. I was a natural salesman so this was going to be a piece of cake. I remember seeing Coach Osborne when the Huskers were in Arizona for the Fiesta Bowl. When I told him what I was doing, he gave me grief by saying, "Yea, I figured you would end up as a used car salesman."

I was determined to be the top new car salesman at this car dealership. I got training and started making sales like crazy. The commissions were a little slim and I became very disappointed to find out how many sales I actually needed to support my family. Just the same, I thought, "No worries I can do this." They had given me a formula for success: X number of opportunities = X number of sales.

After a while I realized that my job was to make people pay too much for a car. That messed with me. I wanted to help people. I was conflicted. One night I actually talked a family out of buying a car because I knew they would be paying too much for it. When I started adding up the time spent at the dealership versus how much money I was earning, I realized that I would have been better off at Domino's.

Respect in the Inspection Industry

Over the next five years I focused solely on building my relationships with Jesus and Carol. It paid off. I was offered a job to start a home inspection business through a contact I had made while in the ministry. I then became a partner with another inspector who was also a Christian. We committed to honoring our wives and making our families our priority.

We established a firm that was centered on integrity and our reputation in the real estate community was impeccable. As we built our business I taught continuing education to realtors. My partner would help write the licensing law for inspectors. Together we became the model for the industry. This kind of teamwork demonstrated to me that when we put energy in the right places there is nothing that can stop a family quarterback.

I am convinced that men can have everything they want, if they will simply surrender to God. Carol and I were able to work out the mortgage on that house. The Lord had allowed us to get the home of our dreams. All this happened because I learned to huddle with a humble heart.

"Delight yourself in the Lord and he will give you the desires of your heart."
Psalm 37:4

Prayer

Dear Lord, lead us away from the temptations of this world. Give us a heart and passion for our wives and children. We believe you are our provider and you will guide us. Amen

CHAPTER 7
CADENCE

I love watching Peyton Manning at the line of scrimmage. To me, he looks like he is orchestrating a symphony. He points, he shouts, he makes hand gestures, he raises his leg, he yells "Omaha," and then finally, he receives the snap. While it may seem like an unnecessary distraction to us the spectators, all of these motions and signals have specific meaning and significance to his teammates.

What is fascinating is, only Peyton and his teammates know the meaning of it all. It is like a secret code. Each team possesses such a code. Each quarterback dispenses this private information to his offense so that they can take advantage of the defense.

In the weeks leading up to Super Bowl XLVIII, reporters were trying to crack the code on Manning's repeated use of the word "Omaha." He said it some thirty-seven times against San Diego in the AFC Divisional round of the playoffs. People in Nebraska were thrilled that their city got so much attention. Meanwhile, everyone else in the country just wanted to know what it meant.

In an interview before the AFC Championship game against New England, Peyton was asked to clarify its meaning. His response was hilarious. "Omaha? It's a run play, but it could be a pass play, or a play action pass depending on a couple of things. The wind. Which way we are going. The quarter. The jerseys that we are wearing. So it varies. Really, play to play."

The play calling cadence is a language spoken to convey specific information for the offense to make the correct blocks, to watch for the correct reads and to adjust accordingly. It can be a combination of numbers, names, and almost anything to convey a particular concept. When I was playing, we used numbers at the line of scrimmage. I might say "fifteen thirty-five fifteen thirty-five hut."

The numbers were not important, unless the first number used was the number of the play called in the huddle. If it was, then by calling the same number, you were actually calling an audible (changing the play). For instance, if the play called was "I right, forty-one, pitch," the play is a pitch to the I-back going right. If I said, "forty-one, forty-nine" at the line of scrimmage, that meant we were changing the play from forty-one pitch to forty-nine pitch, which was a pitch to the left. At the same time, if the play became an audible, then we always went on two. So it would sound like this, "forty-one, forty-nine, forty-one, forty-nine, hut, hut."

We always repeated the numbers, once for each side of the line so everyone could hear the changed call. In every instance, the words had meaning. When the call is being made, it is imperative that the players understand what is being communicated. If they don't, the play breaks down.

Play calling on the field is a football language unto itself. What many do not realize is the language of football goes well beyond the field. That especially is true in the locker room.

There are many unwritten rules for the sanctity of the locker room. One of those rules is confidentiality. Confidentiality is a hallmark of this unique community. What happens in the confines of the team environment stays there. What happens on the field, in the locker room and amongst teammates is supposed to be sacred. For a player to betray this confidence is something this side of treason. I am proud to say that I have heard of few breaches of this trust, among the Husker fraternity. I think this was true during the time that I played at Nebraska because of everyone's loyalty to the team's ultimate leader, Coach Tom Osborne. Protecting the humanity of coaches and players is valuable to a team's integrity as well. I trust that these pages are not violating this privacy. My purpose in sharing these anecdotes is to provide a glimpse into the world of Nebraska football, the lessons I learned and the people who shaped my life.

It is the player's understanding of their place in this community that creates an environment of trust. Humor and teasing are commonly a show of affection within the experiences of any team. These inside jokes are perhaps the most enduring part of these relationships. When former players get together we all remember the common references. Imitating our coaches and mimicking their nuances are the most humorous.

One of my fondest recollections during my brief stint as a graduate assistant coach was being in the coaches' meetings. You realize right away that these guys really like each other. What surprised me was the chief funny man was none other than Coach Osborne himself. For example, we were putting a game plan together one early morning. Defensive backs coach George Darlington was gobbling down some breakfast muffins and crumbs from his meal were falling all around him. Coach Osborne came over and said, "George I think the family of rats hanging out under your chair is starting to get fat. You might have to back off before they get too big." The room busted up with laughter.

The language of love among athletes is teasing one another. It is actually a sign of endearment. Players need to get used to it or they may not fit in. A thin skin is not welcome between teammates. When I married however, I discovered very quickly that this was not a way to show my affection for Carol. Teasing did not work with my wife. She would get extremely offended when I would make fun of her. I now live in a No Tease Zone.

The Play: The Power of Words
"The tongue has the power of life and death."
Proverbs 18:21

According to scripture, we are the people of God, a chosen generation, a royal priesthood. With this in mind, the words that we speak should be a direct reflection of who we are. As the family quarterback, our words can bring life or death to our teammates. We should not underestimate our influence and the impact that we have on those around us.

Words Have the Power of Life
"The mouth of the righteous is a fountain of life." Proverbs 10:11

I have to ask myself all the time "Do my words give life?" As a representative of the Creator of the universe, my words have a lasting effect. My words should be life giving, encouraging, uplifting, and full of grace and mercy. Our surroundings everywhere should be a No Tease Zone.

"The tongue that brings healing is a tree of life." Proverbs 15:4

Wow, our words can bring healing! What a powerful force we possess. Having this ability is like being able to call the perfect play.

"The lips of the righteous nourish many." Proverbs 10:21.

I love this word picture. Obviously our words don't feed the body, so what is being nourished? It's our spirits. It is within our spirits that our words can strengthen, encourage and bring life to all who hear us. What an immense influence we have! We are obligated to take this ability and use it properly.

Words Have the Power of Death

"The tongue has the power of life and death." Proverbs 18:21

We must be aware of the influence our words have over the spirit of anyone we speak to, especially our families. Our wives and children are looking to us to find their value and significance in life. Our expressions toward them will have a profound impact on how they view themselves and God. Our words may seem insignificant on the surface, but they can truly demoralize those in our care.

It's typical for us fathers to use expressions that can be devastating to the spirits of our children:

What We Say	What They Hear
"What were you thinking?"	"You are stupid!"
"Are you kidding me?"	"You are not worth my time."
"You could have done better!"	"You are a failure."
"I have had it with you!"	"Nothing you do is good enough."
"Can't you do anything?"	"You are worthless!"

Just going over these expressions is convicting to me. I know I have said them, and it grieves my heart knowing the damage I have caused.

Probably the best biblical commentary on this subject is in the book of James. James 3:5-11 gives us a great description of how lethal the mouth can be: *"The tongue is a small part of the body, but it makes great boasts. Consider what a great forest is set on fire by a small spark. The tongue also is a fire, a world of evil among the parts of the body. It corrupts the whole person, sets the whole course of his life on fire, and is itself set on fire by hell."*

What a vivid picture this is for us to understand. The tongue—our words, the expressions we use—are a world of evil that corrupts us and sets the whole course of our lives on fire. I have experienced this way too often in my life. I've learned that it doesn't take much to start a fire. For example, a small comment like, "Oh, I guess you are perfect," after Carol shares a concern about my behavior is like touching her with a hot torch. Once the fire is lit, it's hard to put out. By responding to Carol in ways like this over the years, I realize that I have burned down our house so many times it pains me to think about it.

James 3:7 goes on to say, *"All kinds of animals, birds, reptiles and creatures of the sea are being tamed and have been tamed by man, but no man can tame the tongue. It is a restless evil, full of deadly poison."*

We cannot tame our tongues by ourselves, with our own strength. We must be determined to be obedient to God's principles concerning our tongue. We must surrender to the leadership of the Holy Spirit. We must stop ourselves from lighting a fire. If all else fails, gentlemen, we need to just shut up.

I'm reminded of the movie *Bambi*. Thumper is Bambi's rabbit friend, and he says "Momma says, If you can't say something nice, don't say nothing at all!" You know, that really makes sense. Stop the fire before it gets started.

Our Words Come From our Heart (Spirit)

Jesus said, *"Out of the overflow of the heart the mouth speaks. The good man brings good things out of the good stored up in him, and the evil man brings evil things out of the evil stored up in him."* Matthew 12:34-35

So, if I am speaking words that are coarse, hard, bitter, resentful, or judgmental, what does that indicate is stored up in my heart? Do I recognize the condition of my spirit? I must become increasingly aware of the hostility in my spirit. If I am unaware, it will continue to rule my mouth and damage those I love.

The Battle for My Mouth Starts In the Mind

"A wise man's heart guides his mouth." Proverbs 16:23

We are in a fight, a battle to control and defeat our flesh. The struggle we face is to keep our lower nature from using our lips to destroy those around us. This war is for our very lives. If our tongue is a fire, it can burn and destroy. We cannot underestimate its impact and the power it has in our lives. Most importantly, we cannot fight this battle in our own strength.

"The weapons we fight with are not the weapons of the world. On the contrary, they have divine power to demolish strongholds. We demolish arguments and every pretension that sets itself up against the knowledge of God, and we take captive every thought to make it obedient to Christ." 2 Corinthians 10:4-5

Notice who must carry out these actions: *We* demolish. *We* take captive. We don't do this alone. We must draw on the strength of the Holy Spirit. How we think about life controls how we feel in our hearts. This in turn controls our mouths.

I have to draw upon the Spirit of God to show me the changes in my thinking that are necessary. I must learn to surrender my mind to the Spirit of God in me. *"Do not let any unwholesome talk come out of your mouths, but only what is helpful for building others up according to their needs, that it may benefit those who listen."* Ephesians 4:29. This is a great memory verse for each of us. We need to write it on a three-by-five card and let it soak into our souls. It is God's word in our hearts that helps to keep us from sinning against Him.

Like the quarterback who has the plays written on his wristband, we need to write it down so we can remember it. We need to refer to it daily. In this way we can have the help that we need to make the right calls. It will give us the skill to put our teams (our families) in the correct alignment. Our success in the Red Zone depends on it.

We Have to Grow Up. Family Quarterbacking is a Big Boy's Game.

"When I was a child, I talked like a child, I reasoned like a child. When I became a man, I put childish ways behind me." 1 Corinthians 13:11

Ouch! How many of our silly arguments at home are childish? Carol recalls that many of our disagreements reminded her of fights she had with her brother back when she was eight years old. It is so true; we must put away our childish thinking.

There are consequences for underestimating the value of our words. *"I tell you that men will have to give account on the Day of Judgment for every careless word they have spoken. For by your words you will be acquitted, and by your words you will be condemned."* Matt 12:36. In our lives we are the varsity players. The lights are on. The cameras are rolling. Everyone is tuning in to see us play. It's game time. What will be written about us in the newspapers tomorrow?

Reading the Defense:
*"He who guards his lips guards his life, but he who
speaks rashly will come to ruin."*
Proverbs 13:3

How many times have I said things that I wish I hadn't? Countless! I'm sad when I recall the many times I have hurt others with my words. When I was learning how to become a better husband, I realized that I chose the words that came from my mouth so poorly, that I had to write a reminder on my left hand in magic marker. It said, "SHUT UP!" I found it really did help. I needed all the assistance I could muster to help me change my behavior, and this really was useful. Over the years, I have instructed men to try this approach, to see if it would help them as well. One time, I encouraged a man who was struggling to listen to put duct tape on his mouth when having a huddle with his wife. When he tried that she reported, "He finally could hear me."

There are many obstacles we must overcome to train our mouths in righteousness. Here are two to consider:

1. Judgmental Attitudes

We men are wired to be problem solvers. We see the flaws in other people and we are quick to point them out. We also tend to draw quick conclusions, sometimes without all the information we need. This leads to attitudes that can be difficult to deal with.

That was a nice way of saying that we are critical and judgmental. Nevertheless, we need to face the facts: *we are!* Even the most passive of men are just as guilty of this as the outspoken ones. They just don't say the critical and judgmental things they are thinking.

It is imperative for us to recognize these destructive attitudes, arrest them and allow the spirit of God change us. If you are wondering whether or not you have a critical attitude, here is a simple test: Ask your wife. Ask her with a teachable, open heart. Ask her to share with you when she senses that you are being condemning, critical or disapproving with her or the children. If she trusts your willingness to learn and to change, you may be surprised by how often she shares her concerns with you. (This exercise is for serious quarterbacks only! Don't try this if you don't really want to know.)

Our Attitudes Can Actually Teach Us about Ourselves

"You, therefore, have no excuse, you who pass judgment on someone else, for at whatever point you judge the other, you are condemning yourself, because you who pass judgment do the same thing." Romans 2:1

On the way home from our couples' Bible study one night I mentioned to Carol what a jerk one of the other men was for the way he was treating his wife. I pointed out that he didn't even realize it. After pondering my words for a moment she asked me, "What do you think the Lord might be teaching you through him?"

I was dumbfounded by this question. I was wondering what in the world this guy could be teaching me. After I had been struggling with this inquiry for a time she informed me, "You are just like him." OUCH! That hurt. It was the truth, but it hurt my pride just the same.

After discussing with Carol what was going on with this other couple and how it was similar to our struggle, I could see how she was right. I wouldn't have seen that if she had not been willing to be honest. More importantly, I wouldn't have had that experience if I had not allowed her that opportunity to tell me, without my retaliating against her. Being able to do that with the help of the Holy Spirit is a key element of this principle.

Beware of the Quite Critic

Some guys don't speak their judgment against someone else, they just feel it. Unfortunately, their feelings are displayed in their attitudes. Like a toxic waste that can kill those within the vicinity of a spill, so can toxic attitudes deteriorate a loving and caring atmosphere.

This is the spirit of the man described in Proverbs 23:7 (KJV): *"For as he thinketh in his heart, so is he: eat and drink, saith he to thee; but his heart is not with thee."*

This is a great illustration of a man who says one thing but whose heart is saying something very different. Just because we are not verbally expressing our disapproval, disappointment, judgment or criticism, does not mean that our views are not being conveyed.

There are always two conversations taking place. One conversation involves our words while the other conveys our attitudes.

2. Lack of Self-control

In Galatians 5 the apostle Paul makes a list of the attributes evident when people have allowed the Holy Spirit to help them live their lives in a more Godly way. He concludes that list with self-control, something I liken to the exclamation point of character qualities. It is almost like he is punctuating the value of these attributes with the ultimate "flesh killer." What does this list say about our human nature and how often we yield to it? Our need to surrender the control of our lives to the spirit of God certainly includes our mouths.

"Like a city whose walls are broken down is a man who lacks self-control." Romans 2:1. Cities that have no protection are easily influenced, invaded and corrupted by the world. If a man lacks self-control, he is in danger of humiliation and destruction. In football, a quarterback who constantly calls the wrong plays only makes the team's punter work overtime. He never leads the team to a touchdown.

Guarding Our Tongue Leads to Life

"Set a guard over my mouth, O Lord; keep watch over the door of my lips." Psalm 141:3. Protect those who are close to you. Don't let evil corrupt them through you.

"He who guards his lips guards his life, but he who speaks rashly will come to ruin." Proverbs 13:3. Is it possible for us to establish a sentinel that prevents our lips from speaking our thoughts? We must do it. I have been guilty of thinking out loud, and this often ends in tears of sorrow. Many of our family huddles have been derailed by my unfiltered thoughts. Too many three-and-outs and your team ends up on the bench.

"For, whoever would love life and see good days must keep his tongue from evil and his lips from deceitful speech." 1 Peter 3:10. If you want score touchdowns, keep to the game plan. I love the way the way Peter emphasizes personal responsibility with listing *"must keep his*

tongue" in the context of enjoying life. It is up to me to guard my mouth and keep my tongue from evil. This leads to winning.

If It Gushes, Look Out!

"When words are many, sin is not absent, but he who holds his tongue is wise." Proverbs 10:19

"The tongue of the wise commends knowledge but the mouth of the fool gushes folly." Proverbs 15:2

"The heart of the righteous weighs its answers, but the mouth of the wicked gushes evil." Proverbs 15:28

If I'm running off at the mouth it's a pretty good bet something bad will be said. The devil wants us to use our mouths to disqualify us from our position as quarterback. He is determined to render us ineffective and to disable our capacity to lead effectively. *"If anyone considers himself religious and yet does not keep a tight rein on his tongue, he deceives himself and his religion is worthless."* James 1:26

The Red Zone
"Let your conversation be always full of grace, seasoned with salt, so that you may know how to answer everyone."
Colossians 4:6

Although I consider myself to be a very positive person I discovered that I am more corrective, critical and instructional in my conversations with my family than anything else. It actually took reading a dog training book to get my attention.

We bought a Rottweiler puppy when our kids were little. We had previously owned a Doberman pincher so I was familiar with breeds like this that tend to be intense in their demeanor. I wanted to be very intentional in training this dog so the kids could also control it.

The book outlining the Koehler method of dog training was recommended to us. In one section, it suggested that for each correction given to the dog, you should give four praises or affirmations. I was a little shocked to think of this four-to-one ratio. It dawned on me that I didn't even do this with my children. This book wanted me to do it with a dog! That convicted me to start reevaluating how I was engaging our children, Tiffani and Buddy.

From then on I began to evaluate how often I was praising the kids. I learned that my use of correction and praise was way out of balance. Something had to change. I was willing to reevaluate my interactions and start becoming more encouraging. About that same time our couples' Bible study had implemented a project of praising our wives daily. This new focus added accountability. I was able to begin retraining my natural responses.

Learning to affirm Carol was a real game changer for me, especially in light of the weekly accountability in our Bible study. It became an exercise for me to learn to become effective in my communication. I liked the challenge and the results were life giving to Carol and enlightening to me.

The praise project consisted of us husbands verbalizing a positive character quality that we identified in our wives on a daily basis. The intent of the project was to help us begin to see the Lord more clearly in our own daily lives by learning to see the virtues in our wives. As we began to see the goodness of our wives by actively looking for those character qualities, we could learn to appreciate how God had provided for us.

I worked faithfully on this project. As a result I began to see God's goodness and all that He is and does for us. I became more positive with Carol, our children, co-workers, people in general and even the guy behind the counter at the local tire store!

Our families are just waiting for us to fill them with God's love. We have the opportunity to pour grace, mercy and hope into them. This will all come from the words that we use. As our lives become fully focused on the Father's abundance, we can become masters of the cadence. We have the ability, through the guidance of God's Word and the Holy Spirit, to become givers of hope, joy and life. Like Peyton Manning directing traffic at the line of scrimmage to orchestrate the demise of every defense, we can penetrate the darkness of this world by bringing a blinding light to it through the use of words that reflect Christ.

"*You are the light of the world* (the family quarterback). *A city on a hill cannot, be hidden* (under center in the middle of the field). *Neither do people light a lamp and put it under a bowl* (on the bench). *Instead, they put it on its stand and it gives light to everyone in the house* (your home). *In the same way, let your light shine before men* (the cameras are rolling), *that they may see your good deeds and praise your Father in heaven.*" Matthew 5:14-16

Prayer

Dear Lord, "*May the words of my mouth and the meditation of my heart be pleasing in your sight, O Lord, my Rock and my Redeemer.*"
Psalm 19:14. Amen.

CHAPTER 8
LEADERSHIP

I remember the first time I heard a Tony Robbins motivational tape. This guy was so on fire I thought he was going to jump out of my Walkman and shake me. I love listening to men who want to infuse enthusiasm in to others. I'm a huge fan of preachers who pump up a congregation, instilling a can-do spirit in them. We all need these people in our lives.

The trouble is we rarely find men with an attitude like this in real life. When you are giving speeches, screaming into a microphone, or running around a stage, being enthusiastic and motivational is easy. I've done that before, only to get into a huge argument with Carol on the way home from that event. I remember one couples' retreat where we were the keynote speakers. Within minutes after the event we had one of the worst fights of our marriage.

Coach Osborne was one of those men who never got excited about anything. He was consistent and unfazed by circumstance. He was authentic. He spoke truth with humility. He engaged people with genuine love and he made them feel important. He didn't preach it, he just lived it. For example, he always showed up when I was in the hospital recovering from surgery for football injuries.

The leadership lessons I learned that freshman year gave me a foundation that has stayed with me for a lifetime. My most important and memorable example of compelling leadership did not come from any of the superstars on our team. We were loaded with All-Americans, future NFL All-Pros and a Heisman Trophy winner. The player who influenced me the most was our senior co-captain, quarterback Mark Mauer. He had spent his career as a back-up quarterback, waiting patiently for his opportunity to become our starter. Mark's demonstration of leadership has affected me to this day.

That freshman year we opened the season ranked as the number seven team in the country. Our first game was on the road against the unranked Iowa Hawkeyes and Mark was the starting quarterback. We had crushed Iowa the previous year 57-0. On opening day we struggled on offense throughout the entire game and lost 10-7. The folks from Nebraska do not like to lose, especially to Iowa.

The next week we beat Florida State at home and the following game we hosted the number three Penn State Nittany Lions at home, where they handed us a 30-24 defeat. The home crowd was merciless toward Mark. I was in the stands and I could hardly bear the ridicule. We dropped out of the rankings for the first time since 1977. Our 1-2 start was the worst the team had since 1961 and the fans were relentless in their disapproval.

Don't get me wrong. Husker fans are the best in the country. They are educated and respectful of our opponents. In fact, they have been known to stand and applaud a team that can come into Memorial Stadium and defeat their beloved Huskers. They can, however, be less than kind to players who let them down.

The next week we were on the road again to play SEC powerhouse Auburn. We were behind three points at halftime. Coach Osborne could see that he needed to make a change so he took Mark out of the game and started sophomore quarterback Turner Gill the second half. Coach hoped that would infuse a spark of life in the offense. It worked. We scored seventeen unanswered points in the second half and won the game. That evened up our record to 2-2.

Turner became the starting quarterback, and we won the next six games under his guidance. Over his career he would become, in my opinion, the greatest quarterback ever to play at Nebraska. His taking over the team was the launching point that would lead to a 28-2 record, 20-0 in conference play and three straight Big Eight titles. His fourth-place finish in the Heisman Trophy voting his senior season capped his amazing career. In the meantime, Mark did not get discouraged.

Mark's attitude during the 1981 season is the thing that I actually admired the most. He was gracious, encouraging and steadfast. He was a team captain and he continued to perform like one. He didn't pout or act like a victim. He did just the opposite. He led with a great competitive spirit. I'm sure he didn't realize he was influencing me, the freshman, in the way that he was, but his actions now serve as an example to us all.

Late in that season Turner sustained a career-threatening injury while playing against Iowa State. He would miss the remainder of the year. We had risen up the rankings to fifth in the country. Our goal of a Big Eight championship was in the bag and we still had an outside shot at that illusive national title. One obstacle still in front of us was the hated Oklahoma Sooners. We were scheduled to play them in Norman. Mark was going to start again. He had a chance at redemption against Oklahoma. The Sooners had been a thorn in our side for many years, and they were riding a three-game winning streak against us.

At the same time, because of injuries to other quarterbacks, I was able to get a front row seat on the sideline as the number three quarterback. Because Mark never lost focus while he was on the sidelines after being replaced by Turner Gill, and because he stayed engaged in the day-to-day activities of the team while he wasn't a starting quarterback, he was ready to play. He proved to be more than proficient. Mark orchestrated one of the great victories for Nebraska in this historic series between the Huskers and the Sooners. He was eleven for eighteen passing. He ran the offense to perfection and we throttled the Sooners 37-14.

I will be forever grateful to Mark for showing me what true leadership looks like. He wasn't just a talker. He was a man of action. Several years later I remembered his example when I was being booed by the fans and being benched. His example gave me the courage to face the pain of that experience. His example of how to be a patient leader gave me hope that my life's story would not be just about football. He demonstrated that life is much more than that.

I recently discovered that Mark was dealing with some personal struggles of his own. This reminds me that we are all fragile human beings. His example to me as a leader is still valuable for my life. A person's struggles do not remove the good that their lives accomplished. After all, that's why Jesus died—for our redemption.

The Play: Lead by Example
"For God did not give us a spirit of timidity, but a spirit of power, of love and of self-discipline." 2 Timothy 17

To experience a meaningful life-long marriage, we must follow the advice laid out in James 1:22. *"Do not merely listen to the word, and so deceive yourselves. Do what it says. Anyone who listens to the word but does not do what it says is like a man who looks at his face in a mirror and, after looking at himself, goes away and immediately forgets what he looks like. But the man who looks intently into the perfect law that gives freedom, and continues to do this, not forgetting what he has heard, but doing it—he will be blessed in what he does."*

The expression "talk is cheap" resonates throughout all walks of life. The world is sick and tired of hearing people, preachers and prophets *talk* about religion. People are looking for authentic believers who practice what they preach. The world, especially our youth, are looking for Christians who are worthy of being followed. They want no more posers!

The millennial generation is watching to see if the generations before them will do as they say. Young people need to witness genuine love, kindness and grace in action. It's time for us men of God to be living illustrations of the love of Christ and to lead accordingly.

It appears to me that we are losing the culture war because we are hypocrites. If we drag our kids to church and argue with them the entire way, how can we expect them be devoted and obedient to scripture? We demand that they get along with each other, but as moms and dads, we do just the opposite. We treat one another poorly and then expect the children who have witnessed this unchristlike behavior, to be the opposite in their own lives. I have had numerous young couples tell me the thing they fear most about their own marriage is that it will be just like their parents' marriage.

We as husbands and fathers are called to be a living example to our wives and children. This must start with:

Repentance

"Confess your sins to each other and pray for each other so that you may be healed." James 5:16

Every one of us wants our children and spouses to exhibit a repentant spirit, yet where are they going to learn what that looks like if they don't see it in us? If I expect others to have a broken and contrite spirit, and I am not personally familiar with this attitude, how can I teach that to my family? How could I presume that they will be able to learn that from me?

What examples of repentance do you have in your life? When talking with men I have found very few of us who can recall ever hearing our fathers say, "I'm sorry." For anything! With that kind of training it becomes imperative that you and I change our ways if we are to be effective examples for the generations to come. We cannot underestimate the value of turning from our current behavior, making amends with those around us and working to heal the hurts we've caused along the way.

My relationship with Tiffani and Buddy has strengthened because of my remorse over my past offenses. I have shed many tears over my transgressions. That sorrow has helped me to create a greater connections with them. It's the healing that comes from these actions that restores relationships. It is the most relevant ingredient needed to bring rehabilitation to our souls and our families.

Servanthood

"*Whoever wants to become great among you* (family quarterback) *must be your servant.*" Matthew 20:26.

Servanthood is a word that gets passed around like broccoli or asparagus. It's probably good for me, but I'm not sure I'm into it. Many people equate the actions of servanthood to those of the water boy, the equipment manager or the kid who holds your ball cap while you are in the game. We assign such actions little or no significance. In truth, being a servant is what creates credibility in leadership.

Periodically during practices we needed an athlete to fill in to help demonstrate a defensive set or new technique. On more than one occasion Coach Osborne would see that nobody else was filling the spot. Instead of ordering someone else to do it, he would jump in there and execute the needed illustration. We were always impressed with his ability, but more importantly his willingness to humble himself and be like one of us, serving in place of one of his players.

Watching Coach was a perfect illustration of "*serving with joy and gladness...*" Psalm 100:2 (KJV). We get the privilege of laying down our lives for the benefit of others. We get to make the choice to do it with a grateful heart. Servanthood is more than an idea. It is desire, readiness and action. Serving is not a list of chores to accomplish. It's more a lifestyle without expectation.

I have done the dishes a thousand times. If I do them with the wrong attitude, I'm not truly serving. When I have a hidden agenda (like some sort of special reward later that night), or if I'm put off because nobody else did them, I lose the joy of serving. Being a servant requires genuine service. A quarterback who is willing to teach and train those he competes with for his job, earns respect beyond measure. I found unexpected joy in befriending and helping those who were trying to take my job.

Patience

"Being strengthened with all power according to his glorious might so that you may have great endurance and patience, and joyfully giving thanks to the Father, who has qualified you to share in the inheritance of the saints in the kingdom of light." Colossians 1:11-12

I was taught that patience was not having to be in control of life's events. I have also learned that I am never in control of circumstances, only my attitude toward them. The idea that patience is a virtue is an oversimplification. It really is a choice and a manifestation of the Spirit of God in our lives.

Remember patience is listed as fruit that the Spirit dispenses to us (Galatians 5:22). It is the freedom not to react when things don't go your way. A good example is when you ask your son to clean his room, but then you come home and it's still a mess. Do you kindly remind him and maybe even pitch in to help him (servanthood)? Or do you decide to tell him that he is an irresponsible brat? I have done both of these. I can assure you the second method is not the best choice. By name-calling, I was compelled to repent and ask forgiveness of my son because my leadership lacked credibility due to my impatience. Expressing patience is evidence that men of God are embracing the calling that Jesus has made on our lives.

We are able to exhibit patience because we recognize God's infinite grace toward us when He is patient with us. We are the recipients of His patience, mercy and grace. Therefore, we must pass it along. *"But because of his great love for us, God, who is rich in mercy, made us alive with Christ."* Ephesians 2:4

Humility

One of the drawbacks of athletic fame is all the attention a person receives. When people want an autograph and a photo taken with you as a celebrity, you begin to think you are special. There was no bigger celebrity at that time than Coach Osborne. Everywhere we went the masses were waiting. They always wanted a piece of him. A handshake. A photograph. His signature on a program, a hat or a T-shirt. "Can I get an autograph coach?" they would ask. He always took time with them, he talked to them, he gave them a smile and most certainly he made their day. He was one of those unique individuals who made people feel important every time they were with him. His kind of humility has been my goal since my first days in Lincoln. That kind of modesty has a powerful influence on families.

Do our families believe that we "*do nothing out of selfish ambition or vain conceit, but in humility consider them better than ourselves*"? (paraphrased) Philippians 2:3. Humility is a powerful instrument to build confidence in our offspring. To have them know beyond all doubt that they are precious to us is invaluable. Believing that we find interest in them to be more important than interest in ourselves makes them feel special. Knowing that their well-being is our utmost priority, goes much farther than anyone ever could imagine. Just think how the world would be changed if our children believed they could change it, and we showed them how.

Reading the Defense

"How can anyone enter a strong man's house and carry off his possessions unless he first ties up the strong man. Then he could rob his house."
Matthew 12:29

How many of us, like the strongman mentioned above, are tied up, and our wives and children are being defiled and we don't even know it until it's too late? I discovered that I was tied up, and that was when I was in full-time ministry.

I was traveling the world spreading the good news of Jesus, watching people come to Christ by the dozens. I watched believers being "slain in the spirit" when I touched them. Meanwhile, my wife was in tears, hating everything about our life. Not only that, she was planning to leave me. We have shared the sadness of this story to audiences over the past twenty years and invariably we have been approached by couples who are experiencing the same pain and grief.

There is a warning in the third chapter of 2 Timothy regarding those who are posers in their faith. A list of their behavior is compiled, with this conclusion in verse five: *"having a form of godliness but denying its power. Have nothing to do with them."* If the Devil can get us to deny the power of God to show a changed life, the Devil wins. He does not want us to practice godliness. He wants us to be a fake, church goin', hand raisin', judgmental pretender. In doing so, we are tied up, bound and defenseless.

The devil has a strategy to cripple your leadership. That is what he is going to use to tie you up and to sack you. Trust me, because I've been sacked too many times. Learn from me. I was blind, but I'm seeing better these days.

Arrogance

"Pride goes before destruction a haughty spirit before a fall." Proverbs 16:18

If your first thought is "but I'm not proud," that is actually a sign that you are. Denial is the devil's disguised defense. If he can get you looking the other way, that's when you are smacked in the backside.

Here is a quick test: The last time your wife tried to help you discipline the children did it turn into an argument? Or did she recently tell you that your words were hurtful? How did you receive it? Does she help you with your driving? How did you respond? Yeah, me too. The squabble begins! Behavior like that is our sign that maybe we are not as humble as we think we are.

Scripture is full of examples of men in power who could have done well but didn't. They let their prominence get the best of them. They got full of themselves and their position and abused what God had given them. To me, they were first-round draft picks who didn't have the required humility. A great example of this is King Rehoboam. His story is found in 1 Kings 12:7. *"If today you will be a servant to these people and serve them and give them a favorable answer, they will always be your servants."*

The young king was given this charge by the elders of Israel when he became ruler. The elders had served King Solomon during his lifetime and they advised Rehoboam to listen to his people, to care for them and to serve them. He rejected this wisdom and listened to his own friends, who told him to deal harshly with the people. They told him to say, *"My father scourged you with whips; I will scourge you with scorpions."* 1 Kings 12:11b. Rehoboam eventually had to leave the country to save his own life.

This advice is still wisdom today for every husband and father. To lead we must be willing to listen, and receive our coaches' input. This will produce successful results. The way we treat those under our leadership will create either contentment or discourse. It is in our hands to provide an environment of cooperation. I have found in my life that my pride is still the greatest threat to my willingness to illustrate a life transformed by Christ.

Proverbs 14:12 tells us, *"There is a way that seems right to a man, but in the end it leads to death."* Like a quarterback who doesn't read the defense, make an adjustment and change the play, the result is failure. If the defense defends the run to the right and I'm determined to run that way, well, we know what's going to happen. Eventually I'm going to end up on the bench.

I remember a player who was a "weight room All-American." In the gym he looked great in a pair of shorts, strong as an ox, and fast, too. He walked around like he owned the place. His head was the only thing bigger than his biceps. When I inquired about him a coach said to me, "He looks like Tarzan, but he plays like Jane." That guy never saw the field.

Anger

"Be angry and sin not." Ephesians 4:26. *"No temptation has seized you except what is common to man."* 1 Corinthians 10:13

When Carol and I were still dating, she handed me a brochure about issues with anger. I quickly dismissed it and threw it away. She had already seen the red flags in my conduct. I had no interest in discovering what concerned her. She eventually found that brochure, and she still has it. I didn't realize exactly how angry I was until after we got married. My anger was multi-faceted. We will deal with some aspects of that in the chapter "Playing with Pain." I was an angry dude through and through.

The only thing that exceeded the level of my anger was the totality of my ignorance about it. What you don't see, you can never change. A quarterback who doesn't recognize the coverage will inevitably throw interceptions.

I have found that our responses to life are a direct indication of our willingness to let people into our lives to see our "authentic selves." I was scared that if anyone really knew me they wouldn't like me. I am a people pleaser. I can't stand rejection. So naturally I have my defenses up to keep people out. I am finding that my condition is not that unusual. The scriptures above taught me a couple of things about my anger:

- Reacting in anger is a temptation. That means I can make the choice not to give into it. If I do that, I'm in control of this behavior. The anger is not the actual problem either. It's what I do with it that matters.

- Anger can seize me, like when a linebacker grabbed me around the waist and started to swing me around. That monster wants to body slam you. If he could, he would knock you out. There were times that I would get mad for days, weeks, even longer. It's debilitating. Anger is the perfect way to tie up the strong man and throw him to the turf.

No Vision

"Where there is no revelation, the people cast off restraint." Proverbs 29:18

If a leader doesn't know where he is going he is guaranteed to end up right where he is aiming… nowhere. Keeping the family quarterback angry, in dark places, with nowhere to go, plays right into the Devil's game plan. Don't forget he knows you and has a strategy to make you ineffective.

If the enemy can't kill you physically, he will try to take your heart out. The best way to disable an offense is confusion. You see it happen all the time. The opponent brings out a defense that the offense wasn't prepared for. Their game plan goes out the door. If the leader doesn't have vision, there is no direction and the followers have no guidance. Their boundaries disappear.

In the King James Version, it says that *"the people perish."* When the leadership doesn't know where they are going, the team will have to figure it out for themselves. The enemy is just waiting for that. It is when the family is without Godly leadership that the children's faith can end up like the seed on the path where, *"Anyone who hears the message about the kingdom and does not understand it, the evil one comes and snatches away what was sown in his heart."* Matthew 13:19.

As I said earlier, you see this happen when mom and dad are disconnected or divorced. The kids can behave in a fleshly way as well. They can easily divide their parents. When that occurs, the children have even less consistent direction. When parents are not on the same page, their influence diminishes. Imagine if the coaches started fighting on the sideline. We have seen it a few times, even at Nebraska. When that happens, the team tanks, *every time*. I have never heard a player say "our coaches hated each other and that really inspired us to compete."

The Red Zone
"Set an example for the believers in speech, in life, in love, in faith and in purity."
1 Timothy 4:12

If you are expecting this section to be a discourse on my awesome victories in life, or you thought you would perhaps hear stories about my incredible, loving, benevolent leadership, you will be very disappointed. Actually, I wish I could write from that perspective. I can't.

The truth is, I have not met a more arrogant, resentful, and angry man than me. That is why I am so hopeful for every man that I work with. I believe that if God can help me learn how to understand my wife, care for my children and keep a marriage intact, ANYONE CAN DO IT-WITH CHRIST.

I was offered a baseball coaching position with a private Christian school in our neighborhood. I guess they figured I could coach anything because I played college football. For my efforts they gave us tuition for Tiffani. The first week of school Carol was told by the teacher, "all the little studs are glad to have her in class." This was first grade and she was already an object of desire? This was not the environment we were anticipating. One day she ended up punching one of those little studs to get him to stop bugging her. Those boxing lessons I had with her actually came in handy. We opened our Turner Home School Academy the next fall.

Scars
We loved home schooling. Tiffani never went to another school until she enrolled at our local community college when she was fifteen. She graduated from Arizona State University with a Bachelor of Science degree in nursing at the age of twenty. She praises us for our choice. Buddy had a different perspective.

Carol taught the kids daily and we created a twenty-family cooperative that offered us many benefits. We did math at home and Carol added a tutor to help. Buddy's learning style was much different from Tiffani's. He needed a little more oversight and he would often get distracted. Buddy and Carol would butt heads frequently over arithmetic. She tried to manage it all, but as he got older it became more difficult. He was getting bigger and a little more threatening to her. That's when Carol called the vice principle: me.

I was not as patient as I needed to be. I would get frustrated and at least once I threw him in our pool. In January. It cooled him off. On another occasion he needed a firmer hand. I grabbed an available jump rope and spanked him with it. I thought I was following Proverbs 13:24. *"He who spares the rod hates his son, but he who loves him is careful to discipline him."* Well, I clearly missed the "careful" part.

As Buddy grew older he became a state champion swimmer (that's a whole other story). We attended every meet that we could. A year or so after the jump rope incident we were at a swim meet with him. I was standing behind the starting block when I noticed something. He had scars on his lower back. (Here come my tears again). I immediately knew where the scars came from. I had never before noticed the marks that the jump rope left. I didn't remember spanking him that hard or on his back. When I saw the scars, I was mortified. Here I was this man of God who teaches men how to love their families, and my son had wounds on his body from me.

When we got home he was relaxing on our bed watching a movie. I stood over him in tears and told him what I had seen. My heart broke into pieces right in front of him. I couldn't restrain the grief that I was feeling. I cried deeply as I tried to talk with him.

I apologized profusely for my abuse. I acknowledged how that must have affected him and created a lack of trust with me. I told him I didn't want him to fear me like that again, ever. I vowed that I would never treat him with violence again.

I used this experience to shape the way I disciplined him from then on. I did not want that to separate us in our relationship. I hoped that he would see that I would own my offenses and repent. This is why we must confess our sins, so we can be healed (James 5:16). Jesus can set us free. Sometimes we need that.

Prayer

Dear Father, we are inadequate without you. Please grant us your patience as we discipline our children. Give us a vision and a purpose so that we can have a meaningful life. Amen

Chapter 9
Turnovers

My last home game was against the Kansas Jayhawks on November 16, 1985. We came into the game ranked No. 2 in the country. My entire senior season had been a conglomeration of injuries, frustration and disappointment. It had been a difficult year for me and yet we still had a chance to win the conference title and to play for the national championship. Those were our two main objectives heading into the season, and they were still within reach.

I lost the starting job to McCathorn Clayton the first week of the season against Florida State. I stayed focused, played in every game and eventually earned another start six weeks later. As I was getting into bed the night before that road game against Kansas State, my knee locked up on me. When I say "locked up," I mean I could not move it. The instability in my knee had created what the doctors called a "bucket handle" tear in the cartilage. When my knee shifted, it would catch and it was stuck.

The trainers came to my room and unlatched my leg. I begged them not to tell Coach. I had finally earned another start and I didn't want to give it up because of an injury. I think the trainers honored my request.

I started and we played pretty well. We won 41-3. Coach didn't say anything about my leg until after the game. He called me into his office on Monday. He was very kind and genuinely concerned about my health. He told me that we needed to start preparing for Oklahoma. We had Iowa State and Kansas on the schedule before the Sooners. With that in mind, he wanted to get McCathorn and Steve Taylor as much practice and game time as possible.

It was back to the bench for me. I was heartbroken. I really wanted to redeem myself for my poor performance against OU the year before. The truth was I couldn't run. An option quarterback who can't run is not very valuable to the team.

Our last home game was very special. I was proud to be introduced on Senior Day. It was a privilege to be a part of this Nebraska Football program. At the same time it was hard to be so physically limited. My knee was deteriorating by the week. I had torn the anterior cruciate ligament and no amount of tape, braces and injections were going to make me more mobile. I was playing out the season and I was not really looking forward to the impending surgery.

Coach did give me a chance to play. I got into the game late in the second quarter. On the second play, Coach called a pass. I was a little surprised. We were up 31-0 and the ball was on our 18-yard line. The play was I right forty-six iso pass two release. It was a play-action pass designed to suck the defense up and get the wingback to run by the safety. Then I would throw the ball over the top to the receiver. The play worked to perfection, an eighty-two yard touchdown. It was the longest play of the year. This was beginning to be the dream that I had hoped for since my youth: to end the year on a high note.

Real-life doesn't always go according to one's fantasies, however. I was back in the action in the third quarter. We had third and long, so we called a pass play. That was a smart call, because I couldn't run a lick. It was another long pass over the middle.

This time I made the throw too late and the safety came across and picked it off. I was so angry at making the turnover I tracked down the defender who ruined my day and hit him just after he went out of bounds. Oops, I was assessed a fifteen-yard unnecessary roughness penalty. On top of that, my knee totally buckled and locked up on me. I could not even stand up, and I was on the Kansas side of the field. Their players were screaming at me "that's what you get for the cheap shot!"

Ouch! The Kansas players were right. I made my error (interception) even worse by getting a flag (penalty) and hurting my team even more. The most egregious thing was being a poor illustration of Jesus. Some Christian testimony I was.

Adding insult to injury our trainers had to come clear over to the opposing side of the field and practically carry me back to our sideline. After they unlatched my leg I tried my best to talk Coach into letting me back in. I needed redemption. I had to make amends. It didn't happen. That was the end of my football career at Memorial Stadium. My last play in a home game was a turnover with a penalty on top. Not exactly the finale that Disney would write.

The Play: Overcoming Offenses
"The wages of sin is death, but the gift of God is eternal life
in Christ Jesus our Lord."
Romans 6:23

Let's face it: We make mistakes! We get angry. We say things we shouldn't. We forget important dates. We break promises. We can be selfish, thoughtless and uncaring. We make messes, lots of them.

For me it was even worse. I was abusive, violent and unrepentant.

Personal offenses are like turnovers, they are painful but they don't have to be fatal. This is where many of us guys really can struggle. We have a hard time conquering our sinful nature. At the same time, we must honor our wives or children and repair the damage we cause. We must redeem the injuries we have inflicted.

It is critical that we discover the differences between minor negligence and unrepentant sin. It is the later that undoes all our hard work in life, unravels our world, and wreaks havoc on relationships. The enemy of our soul wants to keep us blind to our sinfulness and hold us back from recovery.

I believe that this unrepentant sin is the lack of resolution for a multitude of offenses, and the root cause of many divorces. Learning to heal the damage we cause is a valuable weapon against the forces of evil that want to destroy every Christian marriage.

Avoiding the Fifteen-Yard Roughing Penalty
If you have committed a personal infraction (caused pain to your loved one), the first order of business is don't make it worse by committing another foul. Repentance is the key to healing the offense. There is no other solution. There are however, steps to recovery. I'm not usually a proponent of mechanical formulas to solve spiritual dilemmas. The following steps, however, can be helpful:

1. **Shut up.** Yes, you heard that right. If you are like me, your first responses can be defensive and that's how you end up getting the fifteen-yard roughing penalty. *"My dear brothers and sisters, take*

note of this: Everyone should be quick to listen, slow to speak and slow to become angry." James 1:19. In order to listen, I have to keep my mouth shut. If my lips are flapping, my hearing is not engaged. Then the yellow flags start to fly.

2. **Agree with how the offended person has been affected.** When I hurt my wife, my first reaction is to explain why she should not be offended. This strategy has never worked for me.

   What is more effective is to validate the pain I caused her and acknowledge the wounds I created. This is in accordance with the Apostle Paul's encouragement in 2 Timothy 2:14. *"Keep reminding God's people of these things. Warn them before God against quarreling about words; it is of no value, and only ruins those who listen."* If I do this, I can have the presence of mind to think about the consequences of my actions. Then I can pull up and not get flagged.

3. **Confess your part in the harm you caused.** It is critical that I confess that I did create the injury, even if I didn't intend to. I must admit to the effect I have had on Carol's heart, not what my intent was. If I don't admit what I have done I can never truly recover from the problem that stands between us. *"Therefore confess your sins to each other and pray for each other so that you may be healed."* James 5:16. This is a critical step to overcoming the damage we cause. This is the pathway to healing. It's like picking up the opponent you just fouled and apologizing to him.

4. **Repent.** Change has to happen for restoration to take place. If we go through the first three steps and continue to repeat the offense, it will only embitter your family and create disunity within the house. *"Repent, then, and turn to God, so that your sins may be wiped out, that times of refreshing may come from the Lord."* Acts 3:19. Getting one personal foul can be forgivable. If you keep getting them, you will find yourself on the bench.

5. **Pray.** Hold hands. Seek the heart of the Father by pouring out your repentance to Him. Nothing you do will heal your hearts like earnest prayer. *"The righteous cry out, and the Lord hears them; he delivers them from all their troubles."* Psalm 34:17. This is an essential

ingredient to repairing any offense. I am grateful for His promises when we seek Him.

Repentance = sins wiped out + refreshing from the Lord. Now that's some good play calling. It is up to us to be willing to make that play. We have the ability. When we humble ourselves, there is nothing we can't accomplish. That is called "Winning!"

Reading the Defense
"The reason the Son of God appeared was to destroy the devil's work."
1 John 3:8b

Athletes carry themselves with a unique sense of self-assurance. Sometimes it is a false confidence that covers up their real fears. I call it the peacock effect. If I act as if I know what I'm doing, eventually it might become real.

This same pride resides in the heart of all men. *"The heart is deceitful above all things and beyond cure."* Jeremiah 17:9. We want to be something that we are not. We want to be right. We want to be "The Man." This means we don't want our behavior challenged. We can be deceived into thinking our ways are righteous when they are not. This is the enemy's tool to get us to react when we have caused offenses.

Self-righteousness
My self-righteousness is the preeminent instrument that the devil uses to keep me in disharmony with those I love. If the devil can keep us divided, he wins. He knows that we are stronger when we are unified and more vulnerable when we are on our own.

The best way for him to keep us from examining our own behavior is to allow us to continue to believe there is nothing wrong with how we think, talk and act. Scripture proves that self- righteousness is a part of our human nature that we must scrutinize:

- *"All a man's ways seem innocent to him"* Proverbs 16:2. This verse is very clear about how we view ourselves: Irreproachable. If we believe all our ways are blameless, why would we examine them? With this in mind shouldn't we then examine all of our ways?

Here are some responses to my offensive ways that reveal my innocent self-view:

> "That's not what I meant!" is interpreted as, "Just because you didn't understand what I was saying, it's not my fault."

> "You are being too sensitive!" is heard as, "You should be able to take my painful comments. I did nothing wrong."

> "If you hadn't reacted to me, I wouldn't have gotten angry!" sounds to others like, "You caused me to do it." Note: The real damage here is that our wives will believe us. Wives will reexamine themselves and back off. Then our behavior goes unchecked.

- *"Many a man claims to have unfailing love, but a faithful man who can find?"* Proverbs 20:6. What an indictment, and yet it is so true. How many of us have claimed to be devoted, yet we have not followed through? How many of us have broken promises and acted dishonorably?

- *"There is a way that seems right to a man, but in the end it leads to death."* Proverbs 14:12. This verse has been fulfilled in our lives countless times. I have argued with Carol over the most ridiculous and unimportant issues. These disagreements always lead to pain. In the margin of my Bible right next to this verse is are the words "tears, heartache, remorse." That is what death looks like to me— separation from Carol. When I press for my way it almost always leads to emotional disconnection.

Self-righteousness is not necessarily an overt, easily recognized sin. It can be subtle, reserved, deceitfully disguised. It must be treated as malevolent, vicious and unpredictable. We should take these instructions from Jesus: *"Why do you look at the speck of sawdust in your brother's eye and pay no attention to the plank in your own eye? How can you say to your brother, 'Let me take the speck out of your eye,' when all the time there is a plank in your own eye? You hypocrite, first take the plank out of your own eye; and then you will see clearly to remove the speck from your brother's eye."* Matthew 7:3-5

Self-righteousness is like putting eight two-by-fours laminated together into our own eye. It's a beam the keeps us from seeing straight. It blinds us to everything around us that we need to see clearly.

Mounting Turnovers

It is easy to propel one turnover into a series of mistakes. If we don't repair the first one, the next offense will be more painful than the initial infraction. Multiply this by weeks, months and years and the unresolved conflicts will begin to seem irreparable. This is exactly where the enemy wants to take us. He wants us hopeless. If the devil can get us on the bench, we can't make a play.

Discouragement can lead to carelessness. As the transgressions escalate it becomes harder and harder to see your spouse in her genuine form. Painful interactions turn to spiteful engagements. Indifference begins to set in and it becomes more and more challenging to resolve each error. To make up for one interception, you can start to force other throws. Those usually end up being picked off as well.

Then Fatality Sets In.

Fatality is the hardness of heart described in Ephesians 4:17-19. "*So I tell you this, and insist on it in the Lord, that you must no longer live as the Gentiles do, in the futility of their thinking. They are darkened in their understanding and separated from the life of God because of the ignorance that is in them due to the hardening of their heart.*"

Never, ever underestimate the tactics of the enemy. He focuses his designs squarely on us to destroy us, to harden our hearts and to separate us from a Godly life. He doesn't just want to put us on the bench. He wants to force us out of the stadium entirely.

When "I'm Sorry" Gets Worn Out

There are times when a wife is sick and tired of hearing the words, "I'm sorry," because those words have totally lost their meaning. If I tell my wife I'm sorry for leaving the toilet seat up but continue leaving it up, she no longer believes me. She probably doesn't believe I was ever sorry. If this continues, at some point she may not believe anything I say!

What does being sorry really mean, anyway? I must discover what my family may be hearing when I say those words. Here are a few examples to help you examine your heart. You might even ask your wife if she is hearing any of these when you say, "I'm sorry."

> I'm sorry I got caught, again, doing something I know I shouldn't.

> I'm sorry that you are too sensitive to take my jokes and that you get hurt even though I'm just trying to be funny.

> I'm sorry that we are having this conversation to begin with and I really don't care, but saying "I'm sorry" might just get you off my back.

Misunderstanding Forgiveness vs. Trust

Another tool of the enemy that keeps us off balance is expecting our wives to trust us just because they have forgiven us. There is a major difference between trust and forgiveness. Once a person has genuinely forgiven an offense, it may take some time for them to truly trust again. It is crucial for a man to be patient during the rebuilding process. If major damage has occurred in the relationship, it may take weeks, months and sometimes years, to see the fabric of trust restored.

The enemy wants you to give up, get tired of trying and quit the redemption process. If he gets you to resign, he wins! If he can keep that plank in your eye, he wins! Don't ever underestimate him.

The Red Zone
"Train yourself to be godly."
1 Timothy 4:7b

Lessons We Learned While Lost in a Parking Lot

Carol and I love sporting events, especially if the children of our friends are competing. One evening several years ago we wanted to attend a basketball game at a local high school. This was before smart phones, GPS and all the gadgetry we rely upon now. In truth, Carol is my personal GPS. I often call her CarolStar (like the OnStar™ system in GM products) because she can find anything, anytime. If she has been there once or if she thinks she knows the way, it usually happens. With that in mind we set out to find this school, totally dependent on her knowledge. Well, as you might have guessed, we ended up in a parking lot with no school in sight.

As a way to get directions to the school, I got on the phone to call a friend who was at the game. While I was talking, Carol interrupted and wanted to ask a couple of pertinent questions. I was unable, or unwilling, to hear both Carol and our friend, so I shushed her. You know that put off, don't interrupt me when I'm talking kind of thing! I got the needed instructions from my friend and hung up the phone. With that complete we were on our way. Oh, and "Thank you Lord, it's not too far."

Then I could feel the temperature drop in the vehicle. It was starting to get cooler and cooler (of course, I'm speaking emotionally here) as we pulled away from the parking lot.

Because I was so emotionally in touch and all (LOL) I asked, "What's wrong?" As you might suspect, I received the familiar, "Nothing!" from Carol. Meanwhile, the ice forming on the inside of the car windows told me that "nothing" actually meant "something" and I had better find out quickly what that "something" really was.

I decide to wade into those frigid emotional waters with a casual, "What's up?" I was thinking there's no way she should be upset with me.

This time I was met with the dreaded retort of… Silence. Ouch!

I realized that I'd been around this block a few times; in fact, I'd been down this very street before. Now I needed to navigate my way off this street and I was way too familiar with the dreaded potholes along the way. In the past I had found myself stuck in many of them and I knew it could take a long time get out. Since I was an instructor in "spiritual leadership," I figured I had better start practicing what I preached.

I said to Carol, "No. Really, what happened?" She believed that I was sincere in wanting to know what was causing her distress, so she said, "You haven't done that to me in a long time. I can't believe you did that to me!"

Oh boy. This is usually where the rubber meets the road in life. Facing our offenses is rarely an enjoyable experience. I needed to get through it without getting a roughing penalty (that's how you end up in the potholes along the road). At this point my mind was working overtime and kicked into the "Be careful, don't mess this up, be cool, don't say something you will regret" mode.

I knew what Carol was talking about. I realized that I was "a little short" with her. Her response seemed a little over the top because I wasn't that bad, was I?

So I ran the easy, "I'm sorry, I was short with you," play. I wanted to see if it would work. Uh oh. Nothing. Silence. Oops! It didn't take. She was not buying it.

By that time, my thoughts and my flesh (my lower ungodly nature) were kicking in. The real battle began to take place in my mind. It was a conflict between my flesh (with support from the devil) and me (with the Spirit of God). If I lost, I gave the devil control of my attitude. *"So I say, live by the Spirit, and you will not gratify the desires of the sinful nature."* Galatians 5:24

Here's how the battle played out in my mind:

My flesh: "Wait a second, how can she be mad at you? She is the one who got us lost! I only shushed her. What's the big deal? She's acting like I killed her."

Spirit of God to my mind: "Shut up, don't say it! You will not like where you end up."

My Flesh: "Puleeeeeze, are you kidding me, she caused this."

The Spirit: "Shut up, don't do it. There is a lot more going on here than you know. Try again"

I was really struggling but chose to give in to the Spirit. With my teeth only slightly gritted I said, "I'm sorry." I looked over at Carol, hoping for some sign of hope, maybe a little thawing out. Nope, nothing, nada, incomplete pass. My flesh loved this, so we were back in the battle:

Flesh: "See, It's really her issue. Look at it. First, she got you lost. Second, she interrupted you on the phone. She should be apologizing to you."

Spirit: "Be careful. Don't turn the ball over. Don't fumble! Don't go there, you can't win doing it your way. Don't lose it, you can do it. Try again, don't give in."

The struggle had escalated and I was really trying to hang in there. This seemed too crazy. Just a few minutes ago, we were enjoying ourselves looking forward to watching a basketball game. Now it seemed like we had entered *The Twilight Zone.*

I hated how things had spun out of control, so I decided to throw another pass. "I'm really sorry for being so short with you." I was only slightly less defensive this time but I was hopeful that we could finally move on. I looked over at her and… Nothing! Incomplete pass again!

I began to think it must be time to punt. This is useless. I knew I was going to lose it. This was ridiculous. How could we be this unstable?

The combat in my mind continued:

> Flesh: "You have got to be kidding me, right? Unbelievable! Let's look at this again. If you didn't get it before, first, she got you lost. Second, she interrupted you. Now, third, she doesn't forgive you. You have apologized several times and she hasn't had any of it. This is not your problem. Let her have it, both barrels!"

> Spirit: "Hold on. Don't punt. Stop. Stay in the game. You know better. Take a deep breath. Here is something to consider: You could have handled the whole thing better. You know you were short, you were frustrated at her and you were impatient. You hurt her. She expects better from you. You are capable of so much more."

When I heard those words from the Spirit of God, I knew He was right. Almost instantly, my spirit totally softened. I looked at Carol and said, "I really should have handled that better. I was impatient with you. You don't deserve that. It must have upset you when you to tried to help me while I was on the phone and I got mad at you for trying. I don't want to treat you like that. Will you forgive me for being a jerk to you?"

At that moment she turned to me and everything was different. Her heart was tender toward me because mine was tender toward her. It was an example of "Godly spiritual leadership" at work. She then said, "I'm sorry too for interrupting you. Will you forgive me?" We did, and we both felt refreshed just like Acts 3:19 said we would.

Prayer

Lord, we ask you to forgive us when we sin. Help us see the damage we cause when we hurt others. Father, grant us the grace to repair the wounds that separate us. Lead us to healing and hope. Amen

CHAPTER 10
JUST OWN IT

I can only recall one instance on the football field while playing at the University of Nebraska when I was thoroughly scolded. It happened early in my freshman year. The memory is etched in my mind and affected my spirit as though the event happened yesterday. While I learned a lot during my six years as a player and a coach, this incident probably stuck with me as much as any.

The intensity of our practices and scrimmages were only surpassed by the scrutiny that we received while we were playing. I had never experienced this kind of accountability in my life. Each play was taped. The cameras were always running. There was nowhere to hide from the eye in the sky. We would watch every play, even warm-ups, before the next practice.

When we scrimmaged things would get even more spirited. The stakes went way up because every play was graded like a test. Our standing was based on our grades. We all knew that every play counted, so we had to make the most of every opportunity. Based on our grade we would rise or fall within the depth chart. We were fighting for a job. Tensions ran high. Everything was intense.

The place I could really feel it was in the training room where everybody was taped up before practice. It was usually a jovial spot. On scrimmage days it was a lot more subdued. No one was laughing. There were no jokes. You could cut the tension with a knife. The tape around your ankles even felt a little tighter. Your throat got dry. Your heart rate was already increasing. The trainers tried to make small talk, but you weren't even listening. You felt like your career was on the line

In the locker room I felt like a bull rider getting ready to take the ride of my life. I put my gear on tight. I strapped my shoulder pads down real snug. I made sure I got all the pads in my pants just right. I adjusted my socks perfectly. I even got a new pair of wristbands, because I had to look the part. My sweat towel was tucked neatly into my belt. I was ready.

The particular day of my scolding was one of the last scrimmages before our freshman season started. The competition was fierce. There were six quarterbacks and we all wanted to get as much playing time as possible. The starting job was still up for grabs. One of the competing quarterbacks was a redshirt freshman, so he had experience to his advantage. I had worked my way up to second string, so I had a lot to gain or to lose that day.

I was playing pretty well. We moved the ball consistently when I was under center. I was gaining confidence. I had already made a few nice plays that stood out. Passing plays were uniquely precious because as a team we didn't throw much and our completion percentage was part of our grade.

During one drive it was third down and a pass was called. It was a play-action, drop-back pass with the wingback split to the right, running a square-in pattern. I stepped back, made my read and drilled the ball right to the receiver. It was a perfect spiral headed right on target.

I made the correct read, threw a great pass and the wingback flat dropped the ball. It went right through his hands. Then it was fourth down. I could see my grades declining. My completion percentage was dropping and my chance to start was slipping away. I thought, "My drive is stalled and it's not my fault!"

I looked to the sideline with an attitude of disgust. I shrugged my shoulders with my arms out and my palms up as if to say, "Hey that's not my fault. What do you want me to do?"

Frank Solich was our freshman head coach. He was a fit and fierce five-foot-seven former All-Big Eight fullback who looked like he could still play. I thought he was going to kick my @$$. The veins were popping out of his neck and his face was bright red. He came at me like a man who had lost his mind. I had never seen him react like this. He started screaming at me, "Don't you ever show up your teammate. You take responsibility for yourself and never ever blame anyone else. You are a quarterback, act like it!" I hung my head and headed to the sideline. I knew he was right, and I was embarrassed.

This incident served me well on the football field and, more importantly, in life. Learning to take responsibility in spite of circumstance has been of great value. The willingness to "just own it" is a quality that produces special dividends. While the films would show that I did my part during that play, it didn't reveal the genuine life lesson that I gained.

The Play: Take Responsibility
"...the husband is the head of the wife as Christ is the head of the church"
Ephesians 5:23a

The quarterback is expected to take responsibility for almost everything that happens on the field. At all times he must be willing to handle himself with poise, patience and resolve. If this is true of a football player, how much more is expected of a family quarterback who is responsible for his wife and children? It is imperative that we grasp the enormity of this task! *We* are God's representative. We need to show His love, kindness and patience to our families. We have been given this responsibility. We must use it wisely. At the same time this endowment also has liability. *"From everyone who has been given much, much will be demanded; and from the one who has been entrusted with much, much more will be asked."* Luke 12:48

We must not take the role of spiritual leader lightly. We are called to demonstrate the love of God that is in Christ for those under our care. We are no longer living our own life. *"I have been crucified with Christ and I no longer live, but Christ lives in me. The life I live in the body, I live by faith in the Son of God who loved me and gave himself for me."* Galatians 2:20

Our love for our families is to be unwavering, unconditional and inseparable, like the love of Christ. It is our obligation to experience and illustrate this unchangeable love. *"Who shall separate us from the love of Christ? Shall trouble or hardship or persecution or famine or nakedness or danger or sword?"* Romans 8:35. *"No, in all these things we are more than conquerors through him who loved us. For I am convinced that neither death nor life, neither angels nor demons, neither the present nor the future, nor any powers, neither height nor depth, nor anything else in all creation, will be able to separate us from the love of God that is in Christ Jesus our Lord."* Romans 8:37-39

We are responsible to step on the field of life, huddle up, take the snap and execute the playbook. This is a privilege endowed to us by our creator. It is inherent to our position as family quarterback to exhibit the needed maturity when applying our leadership.

We are to be like Christ for our wives and families. They should experience:

- Consistent connection, a feeling of love, and value that stays with them even during trouble, hardship and persecution. Even when they are behind on the scoreboard and the game is slipping away, they should feel connected to and supported by us.

- Confidence in our love for them as they experience trials, tribulation and struggle. When they aren't playing well, miss blocks and line up incorrectly, that confidence should remain.

- Unfaltering affection regardless of circumstances, behavior or performance. When they drop passes and get unnecessary penalties, our affection remains.

We are quarterbacks. We must act like it. We keep our heads up, focus on the creator and gain wisdom from the playbook. Everyone is watching and looking for guidance. Nobody else is going to lead our families to the promised land of peace and joy. The coach is calling our number, the ball is in our hands; the choices we make will direct the course of our lives.

"I urge you to live a life worthy of the calling you have received. Be completely humble and gentle; be patient bearing with one another in love. Make every effort to keep the unity of the Spirit through the bond of peace." Ephesians 4:1a-3. We have been granted a great calling as a husband and father. We are expected to act worthy of the high honor we have been given. We are responsible for expressing patience, humility and commitment to harmony.

Eye in the Sky

Watching film daily was an accountability that always enhanced our future performances. It was invaluable to review the tape and discover nuances that could be corrected. We made major and minor adjustments because of the insight that the tapes revealed. The eye in the sky did not lie. It revealed the truth that we needed to lead us to consistent success.

My huddles with Carol and the kids often turned into something akin to a film session. We would review life's events, discern the value of our experiences and learn from our mis-steps. Replaying our lives became a habit that is with us to this day. It allows us to enjoy the details of our lives. These special moments create a celebration of the goodness that God brings into our lives.

Just like watching an option play that works to perfection and ends in a touchdown, we want to rewind our life highlights as well. Take a minute and enjoy those special moments. We will never regret spending time reminiscing about small and large victories. The challenge comes when the play breaks down. When you fumble, make an interception, or turn the wrong way, watching those plays can be hard to take unless you intend to learn from them. This is even more difficult when it comes to our personal lives. Rewinding our painful interactions has great reward if we are willing to take time to be teachable.

Learning from Our Offenses: Advanced Application

This chapter is a continuation of the chapter on turnovers. In that chapter I described the process of overcoming our offenses. Now I will give you the deeper application of that play. For us, the true value of repentance is discovered during our film session.

When Carol and I would go through a painful event in our family life, often I would see that I created the pain. By reviewing those events and seeing how I caused the pain, I was able to gain understanding, ask for forgiveness and allow for healing. For instance, when Carol and I talked two days later regarding the circumstances we encountered in the car when we got lost on our way to a basketball game, it comforted her when I proposed to learn from that experience. We huddled up and replayed that evening. She was able to express the hurt I caused when I was so impatient with her. She described how close we were at the time and how my attitude toward her made her doubt my love. She was honest and vulnerable. I owned up to the injury I had caused. I reassured her of my commitment to respect and love her. She said that she recognized the struggle I was having. She expressed gratefulness for the self-control that I did exhibit.

From those events I learned that I have to watch my attitudes very closely, all of the time. When our lives become tightly entwined with one another, there is a special bond. That oneness can be tested with the smallest of offenses. Those offenses, if left unchecked, will create disconnection.

We both benefit from rewinding the negative plays. I discover the intricate effects of my actions on Carol and the kids. This also reassures her that I am not apt to make the same turnover again. Carol and the kids become more familiar with my willingness to guide them into peace and joy. Everyone wins. It's up to me accept the mantle of family quarterback and the responsibilities that go with it.

Reading the Defense
"...men are without excuse"
Romans 1:20b

After that scrimmage my freshman year our film session was the next day. I was nervous waiting for the fateful play that led to my life lesson. We reviewed the play several times. Coach Solich praised me for my decisions and the throw I made. He said nothing about the dropped pass. He simply looked at me with that, "now you know how to act" look. His message was concise and clear.

The principle of taking responsibility is perhaps the most difficult concept I have ever tried to convey to others. Over the years I have spent countless hours in private sessions and seminars trying to convince men that as God's representative we are responsible for the health and wellbeing of our family. This is a vital conviction for the family quarterback to embrace. The prince of darkness is not going to let you grasp its value without a fight.

There are two major habits that men must overcome if they ever are to experience the full capacity for which God has ordained them.

1. The Habit of Blaming Others
Like my shrugging and throwing my hands up, my first natural response to anything that holds me accountable is to point the finger at something to get the focus off me. This is a typical reaction. Unfortunately, it never leads to resolution, connection or unity. It usually leads to a debate regarding who started it, what day it was, when it actually happened, or anything else to deflect my actually taking ownership.

The main stumbling block for most men seems to be the disparity between fault and responsibility. For me, I had to resolve that it just doesn't matter. Like that day on the football field, it was not my fault the receiver dropped the ball. It was my responsibility to make the most of it, encourage him, let him know "it's okay. We'll get 'em next time." It was my job to keep my head up and act like a quarterback.

This was not an issue for Jesus. He did not go to the cross because our sin was his fault. In fact, he was sinless. If anyone could hold us in contempt and incriminate us, it's Jesus. Yet, *"He himself bore our sin in his body on the tree, so that we might die to sins and live for righteousness."* 1 Peter 3:24. Without any fault, he bore the responsibility of our sins. His example of taking responsibility was to pray while hanging on the cross, *"Father, forgive them, for they do not know what they are doing."* Luke 23:34. He was interceding for the men who tortured, stabbed and pounded nails in his hands and feet.

If that had been me I would have argued and defended my actions. We are to demonstrate the same grace and mercy that allowed Christ to die for us. We are called to share that unconditional love with the world, and in particular, with our families.

2. The Habit of Making Excuses

I like to call making excuses a case of the "yeah, buts." It's easy for a man to create alibis, defenses and justifications. These "yeah, buts" keep us from acknowledging the impact we are having. When I'm working with a man to help him take his God-given role of responsibility and lead his family regardless of what he sees as "their issues," I remind him of the "yeah, buts."

"The wrath of God is being revealed from heaven against all the godliness and wickedness of men who suppress the truth by their wickedness." Romans 1:18. In my family my excuses and defensiveness were godless and wicked. I was suppressing the truth of the damage I was causing by defending my actions. This wrath was revealed when Carol left me and took with her what was most precious to me: our kids.

"Since what may be known about Gods is plain to them, because God has made it plain to them." Romans 1:19. God's ways have been taught to us. We memorize verses. We attend Bible classes. There is nothing that is not available to us, yet we continue to deny His power and influence in our

lives by defending our behavior and not expecting more from ourselves. Is it possible that God's wrath looks like the arguments we have over small, silly things?

"For since the creation of the world God's invisible qualities-his eternal power and divine nature-have been clearly seen, being understood from what has been made, so that men are without excuse." Romans 1:20

Rejecting the Replays

To work through our conflicts and wounds, our wives may bring up the fights and disagreements we have had. They truly want to resolve them and reconnect with us. They feel this distance from us and their motive and desire is unity. My inherent response is to reject these healing opportunities. Nothing in me naturally wants to review my angry, defensive reactions. I can even use scripture to defend my unwillingness.

It was common for me to accuse Carol of lack of forgiveness if she brought something up. This revealed my lack of understanding regarding the difference between forgiveness and forgetfulness. God himself does not forget. Just look at those pages between Genesis and Revelation. You will find that God documented the offenses of men throughout history for us to learn from. The Creator wants us to be impacted by the past. If we reject the replays, we miss the wisdom, insight and adjustments that they can teach us. We can gain valuable insight if we don't let the devil keep us from review. I have not forgotten the lessons I learned during that scrimmage more than thirty years ago.

Red Zone

"...if anyone does sin, we have an advocate with the Father—
Jesus Christ, the Righteous One."
1 John 2:1b

Jesus illustrates an advocacy that we can use to help us. If we could understand our ability to stand in the gap as He did, we would be able to defend and "cover" those we love. If we could set aside blame and excuse making, we have within us the capacity to *"love each other deeply, because love covers a multitude of sins."* 1 Peter 4:8

Many years ago when our children were very little our lives seemed out of control. We were hustling to make ends meet with different business opportunities. We were home schooling, and though it was extremely fulfilling, it was exhausting. On top of all that, our personal lives were still healing and I was learning the hard way how to love and lead with grace.

Our schedule was so hectic we were not always able to make the birthday parties, showers, and other gatherings our friends would invite us to. Sometimes we would fight on the way to these events and Carol wouldn't feel like going because "she didn't want to fake it." Often we would go home and try to work through whatever that day's dilemma was. This was also the case when some of Carol's friends would arrange play dates for the kids.

Our erratic attendance record became an issue for one couple in particular. We had missed several events over time. The wife's parents got involved because they were also part of our lives. They wanted to mediate, so they asked Carol if she could get together with them to try to resolve these perceived offenses. I had witnessed the results of these types of "get togethers" before and they rarely went well for Carol. So, I invited myself.

When the meeting started I made it known that I was representing Carol (who was sitting right next to me) and whatever problem they had with her, they had with me as well. I explained that I am the leader of the family and I am responsible for any misbehavior that may or may not be taking place. My goal was to protect Carol from accusation. The couple listed several examples of Carol not attending play dates, birthday parties and other events. I listened to their concerns, allegations, bitterness and hurt. I assured them that our lack of engagement was not intentional. I took the opportunity to apologize and honor their disappointment.

I let them know that Carol's inability to follow through was due to my lack of leadership. I explained that I was not caring for her properly, or loving her like Christ would. I said that our lives were so out of control that Carol didn't have chance to be a proper friend. I told them we were very focused on resolving our personal conflicts and that our relationship was our main priority.

They accepted our apology with an understanding that I was responsible for these misgivings, not Carol. This meeting became a milestone of sorts for us. It may have been the first time I actually showed responsibility for our relationship. It was painful, uncomfortable and challenging. Yet, it strengthened us, and gave Carol an immense amount of hope. She felt loved. It provided us with an illustration of authority, headship and advocacy. She would say that I laid my life down for her, as Christ would.

When we stand our ground and act like a quarterback, our families will feel understood, supported and protected. This is our calling. Just own it!

Prayer

Dear Lord, you are our great advocate, thank you. We need your intercession. Give us courage when want to blame and excuse ourselves. Help us follow your example. Amen

Chapter 11
Teammates

The bond between athletes is undeniable. They build a special connection because they spend so much time together. They produce indelible memories and even years later, shared stories are vivid and special. Coach Osborne always emphasized to us that relationships were a valuable commodity we would take away from our time in Husker Nation. I now understand what he meant.

One of my very best friends to this day is Craig Sundberg. We shared the starting quarterback position my junior year. He was a senior and had spent four years behind Turner Gill. After Turner graduated Craig finally got his shot. A shoulder injury hampered him early in the season. After he had a difficult game against Oklahoma State, Coach gave me my first start. The day he told me, I was actually more sad than excited.

Craig had become a friend and I hated to see this happen to him. He handled it with maturity and grace. His father, Dave, even wrote me several letters of encouragement. This exhibition of character and class only enhanced our relationship. Craig was supportive and helpful during the course of the year. Our friendship grew to the point that he stood up for me as a groomsmen when Carol and I got married. I still like to give him grief that I didn't even receive an invitation to his wedding the previous summer.

Craig and I talk regularly. When we travel back to Lincoln, he and his wife, Nancy, often invite us stay in their home. His parents, Dave and Linda, treat us as if we are family. They make us feel like we are at a home away from home. They have been supporting our ministry endeavors as well. Friends like these are priceless.

This is what Jesus was talking about when he said, *"Give, and it will be given to you. A good measure, pressed down shaken together and running over, will be poured into your lap."* Luke 6:38. This value is found in our most precious resource: relationships.

Some relationships are established in difficult times. Those tend to last a lot longer because they have been tested and tried. We benefit from the struggles we experience together. Like iron forged by intense pressure and heat.

Other relationships are created by conflict and remorse. My senior year was a roller coaster physically and emotionally. I shared earlier that I lost the starting position, got it back, then my leg failed me and I was on the bench again. Heading into our final home game against Kansas I was not a very happy camper. I was frustrated with my condition and the course of the entire year.

Early in the week before we played the Jayhawks, I had a regrettable encounter with another player. I don't clearly remember the circumstances that brought it about. I do recall getting into a verbal altercation that turned into a shoving match in the locker room with wingback Von Shepherd. I lost my temper, grabbed his shirt and it ripped.

My pride is not easily subdued. It took a couple of days and a little prompting (okay, a lot of prompting) from Carol for me finally to apologize to Von. I asked his forgiveness and gave him a few dollars to replace his shirt. We had always been friendly in the past. He forgave me and we hugged it out.

Remember the story of that Kansas game I shared earlier? Guess who was on the receiving end of the eighty-two-yard touchdown pass? None other than Von Shepherd. It was the longest scoring play in several years of Nebraska football. We were able to share this special time together only because we made amends with each other. We laughed about it after the game. I couldn't help but believe it was a blessing from God. That kind of tale only happens with the mercy that He offers us.

The stories that we write with our lives include all of our teammates. Those people are the ones who witness our various trials, turnovers, touchdowns and victories. They can tell of the accounts of God's mercy and grace as we allow them to change us.

The Play: Building Unity with Teammates

"I no longer call you servants, because a servant does to know his master's business. Instead, I have called you friends, for everything that I learned from the Father I have made know to you."
John 15:15

Creating an environment for relationships is easy on a football team. You are stuck together for hours at a time. You live, eat, practice, huddle and compete together all year. You gravitate toward those who play on your side of the ball. You spend the most time with those who also play your position. You are also competing with those guys, which can make for some shaky relationships.

The position of quarterback has unique demands that require lots of extra study. Quarterbacks are expected to understand all of the offensive positions. This is the same for family quarterbacks. We need to have a thorough working knowledge of our wives and children. This may seem elementary, yet it is actually very intricate. You may have heard the comment, "Nobody can understand a woman," or seen the picture of a complicated instrument panel with the line, "this is how to operate a woman," while the panel for men has just one or two switches.

Understanding the Mind of a Woman is a Required Skill Set

As a quarterback you need good feet, a strong arm and the ability to make quick good decisions. In the same way, the family quarterback must be able to discern the minds and emotions of his teammates. Having good feet for dancing, a strong arm for throwing the kids in the pool and the willingness to make good decisions are also bonuses.

In the chapter on the huddle we discussed the time needed *"to live with your wife in an understanding way."* 1 Peter 3:7 (paraphrased). Our willingness to clearly and knowledgably engage with our wives is not a suggestion, it is compulsory. This is true for our children as well. Everyone on our team is growing, maturing and changing daily. We have to keep pace. Like a game plan that gets adjusted week by week, our playbook gives us insight into the diversity of each position. In scripture, we are also given wisdom into the motivations of all the players. *"We have different gifts, according to the grace given us."* Romans 12:6a. The gifts mentioned here are the motivational inspirations, or spiritual endowments for each person. It is like the driving force, or the God-given desire. Psychologists call these differences "personality." Scripture refers to them as gifts.

The apostle Paul continues with his instruction regarding teammates with, *"If a man's gift is prophesying, let him use it in the proportion to his faith. If it is serving, let him serve; if it is teaching, let him teach; if it is encouraging, let him encourage; if it is contributing to the needs of others, let him give generously; if it is leadership, let him govern diligently; if it is showing mercy, let him do it cheerfully."* Romans 12:6b-9

It is my understanding that each person has only one of these specific gifts. It is as if Paul was giving us a breakdown of the players, their skills and strengths. I am going to break down each position for you to help clarify what I mean. It is advantageous to understand our teammates. Perhaps this roster will be of assistance.

Romans 12:6-9 lists seven gifts for us to consider. I hope that you can see yourself and your teammates in this list of gifts. Here is a very brief description of the gifts and a list of characteristics that go with each. This is not comprehensive, but it comes from years of studying people and their responses to life:

- **Prophesying**
  The prophet is not a fortune teller. Prophets distribute information in detail and with vigor. A good example might be a "Fire and Brimstone" preacher. Fearless, uninhibited, strong convictions, verbal, strong opinions, critical mind.

- **Serving**
  The servant works tirelessly behind the scenes. A sound tech at church may be a servant. Prepared for anything, knowledgeable, a mind for details, willing to be obscure.

- **Teaching**
  The teacher loves to study, research and acquire deeper meanings. The college professor with multiple degrees fits that gifting. Serious nature, quick minded, self-disciplined, great story teller, social misfit.

- **Encouraging**
  The encourager, also called an exhorter, enjoys helping others reach their goals. An encourager might be an evangelist, a motivational speaker or a Realtor. Playful, entrepreneur, spontaneous, quick friend, class clown, thrill seeker, disorganized.

- **Contributing**
  The contributor, or giver, uses his or her resources to enhance projects. Philanthropists and major donors have this gift. Business success, generous, calculated, focused, pride in giving.

- **Leading**

  The leader, sometimes called a ruler, organizes strategies for the best outcomes of everyone in an organization. The chairman of the board, CEO and, in my opinion Coach Osborne may have this gift. Successful, deliberate, planned, structured, efficient, orderly, serious.

- **Showing Mercy**

  The person gifted with mercy cares for the affect that life has on each individual. Social workers and nurses come to mind. Thoughtful, cautious, engages social issues, inconspicuous, lacks natural confidence.

The above is just a small sampling of the qualities each gift expresses.

Many things in our lives affect our personalities. Those elements combine to create our responses to life. When building unity with teammates, it takes a thorough understanding of who they are and how they behave. As we gain that understanding, our ability to influence them increases rapidly.

In addition to gifts, other influences also help to determine who we are. This is a partial list of some of those influences:

- **Birth Order**

  I am convinced that this is a critical component of our behavior. Firstborns tend to be more naturally responsible than the baby of the family. The middle children will experience life in response to their siblings.

- **Training**

  Our parents, their personalities and their training, will affect how we are raised. An organizer father will train his offspring to be detailed.

- **Disposition**

  The extrovert and the introvert will express themselves differently. This may be a by-product of a person's gift, or it could be a learned behavior.

- **Economic Environment**

  The impact of financial circumstances, whether rich or poor, cannot be underestimated.

Knowing these valuable considerations will help us create a positive environment in our homes. Our teammates will feel like we know them. We will have a much clearer ability to guide and direct our team when they believe we understand them. The feeling of being understood is powerful. *"We do not have a high priest who is unable to sympathize with our weaknesses."* Hebrews 4:15a

Another benefit of knowing our teammates is that we won't react in ignorance. When we have perspective about one another's personalities we are able to respond with kindness. We won't be caught off guard by other's behavior. We can even anticipate the struggles our teammates may experience. *"Carry each other's burdens, and in this way you will fulfill the law of Christ."* Galatians 6:2

As the family quarterback the burden of creating teammate unity is in our hands. Getting into a fight with your wingback will not create the harmony that you desire. It is our distinct obligation to generate a spirit of cooperation, familiarity and compatibility. The apostle Paul instructs us emphatically, *"I urge you to live a life worthy of the calling you have received. Be completely humble and gentle: be patient bearing with one another in love. Make every effort to keep the unity of the Spirit through the bond of peace."* Ephesians 4:1b-3

Live a worthy life. Be humble, gentle and patient. Make an effort to keep unity with your teammates, through peace. Be the family quarterback you are called to be.

Reading the Defense
*"Do not be afraid of what you are about to suffer. I tell you,
the devil will put some of you in prison to test you."*
Revelation 2:10a

This instruction from Jesus can give us the proper warning that we need. There are tests coming our way. God permits the devil to help train us.

Our coaches would often put us into situations during practice to prepare us for the opponents we would face. This would make us more familiar with the defenses, blitzes and alignments. This training would serve us well.

Because unity is such a valuable commodity to the believer, your opponent the devil is not going to tolerate it. He is going to put up as many obstructions in life as he possibly can create. Conflict and division are his weapons to destroy the fabric of unity in our homes and our churches as well.

We must keep our eyes open for the components of destruction our foe will attempt to use against us.

Expectations

When Carol and I started getting serious in our relationship, she asked me what my expectations were. I had no idea what she was talking about. I didn't know myself well enough, so it was easy to say, "Nothing." A lack of awareness is the opponent's best friend. If we don't see it coming, we are going to be subject to it.

I ran straight into *my* expectations early in our marriage. During the honeymoon it became obvious that my assumptions were prevalent, explicit and dynamic. The most endemic presumption I had was sexual. I was under the impression that Carol would fulfill my sexual inclinations without question. I got a quick awakening in this area. I was not happy about it.

My first major offense came when I asked her to go into a bar where we would act like strangers so I could flirt with her and pick her up. She was hurt by this suggestion and she asked me, "How many girls did you do that with? I don't want to be like them." I thought my intensions were innocent, but clearly, they weren't. This was a sign of things to come for me. I would learn over the course of time that my sexual thinking was more erotic than intimate. I created an atmosphere of unhealthy sexual expectation that would take years to overcome.

Sex is the most common cause of disconnection in married couples. I call it the elephant in the room. If this elephant isn't trained properly it will destroy the fabric of grace, kindness and unity that holds a couple together. As you can see, a willingness to address our "sexpectations" is imperative.

Our other preconceived notions go well beyond sex. They intertwine into almost every area of our relationships. Who is going to clean house? Who takes care of the kids? What kind of school do our children attend? Who is going to balance the family budget? This list is endless. It is imperative that we huddle up, communicate graciously, get the snap and have a game plan for all of these obstacles. "*I appeal to you, brothers, in the name of our Lord*

Jesus Christ, that all of you agree with one another so that there may be no divisions among you and that you may be perfectly united in mind and thought." 1 Corinthians 1:10

Need for Control

If expectations don't keep you at odds, then the battle for control might get it done. Every team tries to dominate and control its opponent. This can also happen within a marriage. In an effort to exert a man's "rights," a family quarterback can become demanding. These demands will be met with strong resistance from those under his care. Like sand sifting through his fingers, a man will find this conduct to be ineffective.

When a husband has good cause for the direction his leadership is taking the family, he must implement his leadership with mercy. If he doesn't, a tug-of-war may ensue with his wife or children. These battles typically end with everyone feeling disconnected. Animosity results and the devil completes his objective.

If altercations continue, a man may resort to a biblical consideration to get his way. He may play the "you must respect me" card. Unfortunately, this is not the respect scripture requires when it says, *"Wives must respect her husbands."* Ephesians 5:33b. This interpretation is a "don't challenge me, my opinions or my direction," derivative of respect. I have tried this ploy and it never resulted with others honoring me in an authentic way. When we lovingly, patiently, tenderly, cooperate with one another, we acquire admiration. Respect cannot be demanded, it can only be earned because of respectful leadership.

The struggle for control really resides in fear. There is an abundance of issues that cause fear in us family quarterbacks. I have become a huge fan of researcher Brene Brown. She is famous for two separate TED talks. Her book *Daring Greatly* is having an enormous impact on my life. In her research, she found that men's greatest fear was to appear weak. When I first heard this, I thought she was way off. We are more complicated than that, I thought. I decided to try it out on my clients and myself. I quickly realized she was dead on.

This realization helped me discover a deeper struggle we are experiencing. The apostle Paul was contending with a "thorn in his flesh." He pleaded with the Lord to have it removed. *"But he said to me, 'My grace is sufficient for you, for my power is made perfect in weakness.'"* 2 Corinthians 12:9a. We fear weakness, yet it is weakness that perfects the Lord's power in us. Our fear keeps us from the Lord. It is our weakness that allows His Spirit to be strong, powerful and influential, in and through us. We must do the unnatural: We must embrace our weakness, not fear it.

Unforgiveness

If our enemy can't get us with a blitz of expectation or control issues, he will use the constant barrage of unresolved conflict to do the job. This strategy will slowly separate family members. It will render a family unwilling to engage, frustrated and void of fellowship. We all know stories of disconnected families that seem to have lost the joy of their relationships.

We have the capacity to hold grudges for days, weeks, months, years and even decades. I have members of my own family who refuse to talk to one another. The wounds are deep, unresolved and debilitating. It delights the devil to see us at odds. He rejoices in our suffering.

This kind of disconnection is the purpose for our huddling to help prevent our turnovers. We are required to, *"make every effort to live in peace with all men and to be holy; without holiness no one will see the Lord. See to it that no one misses the grace of God and that no bitter root grows up to cause trouble and defile many."* Hebrews 12 14-15

The willingness to be forgiving starts with the family quarterback. As the leader, we are to exhibit the ability to build unity. This skill can be passed down from generation to generation. We can affect our heritage by resolving all our conflicts.

The Red Zone
"I have given you authority from heaven. I have given you authority to trample on snakes and scorpions and to overcome all the power of the enemy; nothing will harm you."
Luke 10:19

These are strong words from Jesus to the faithful. He has given us authority. I'm not sure about dealing with snakes and scorpions, I suppose that could come in handy, but I'm going to pass on testing that ability.

However, by using His authority and the power of the Holy Spirit, I would like to tame my tongue, arrest my flesh and lead with grace.

Sunday mornings seem to be the most opportune time for God to teach me lessons on unity and conflict resolution. These lessons rarely have to do with church, sermons or potluck dinners. On Sundays, the whole team is together, our lives are clashing and the need for cooperation is high. The lights are bright, it's game time and it's time to get your helmet on and step onto the field.

One particular Sunday a lesson was in the making and I had no idea what was about to hit me. I have found that The Holy Spirit loves to intervene at the most suitable time. He is a gentleman when He instructs. He will speak our special language to make His point, yet is up to us to listen, receive and call the perfect play.

Our family was running late for church as usual. The kids were teenagers, Tiff was sixteen and Buddy fourteen. At least they were old enough to get themselves dressed and ready. As we were we trying to hustle out the door, we were waiting for Tiffani. The rest of us were in the kitchen when she came out of her room. As soon as I saw how she was dressed, I knew there was going to be a problem. If you have daughters, you know exactly where this is going.

She was stylishly dressed as always. She is a beautiful girl. She was, however, wearing a slightly snug pair of white pants. When she was given these pants a few weeks before this event, I had already started dreading the inevitable confrontation. When I saw what she was wearing, I immediately ordered her to "turn around and get something more appropriate on." She indignantly went back into her room slamming the door behind her.

I thought, "This is my job. I need to protect her from wearing things that are not modest. I'm doing a good thing here. I'm being a good leader." I looked at Carol with a "Why is she getting so upset with me?" glance. She responded with, "Why are you mad at us?"

This reply totally caught me off guard. It seemed like an undeserved penalty flag. A couple of things caught my attention. First, she included herself (us) in her comment and second, she said I was mad. I gave her the "What!?" glare. She replied to my indignation with, "we don't know, please be patient with us."

I had to read the defense. I expected Tiffani just to obey me without having an attitude. I wanted to defend myself but I knew that never goes well. I was afraid of losing control of the situation. I wanted to make excuses, but that always ends in tears. I started to check my heart. Carol was right (as usual). I was angry. I didn't think things were that bad, but she could tell I wasn't being patient. I know that my anger is threatening to everyone.

This beam (my anger) needed to be removed from my eye before I could do speck removal (correcting her wardrobe) from Tiffani's eye. I kept my mouth shut. I started to think and pray. I began to see that I had anticipated the friction that getting ready for church can create. I was already pent up with anxiety. I absolutely hate conflict and dealing with discord is not a strength of mine. It's like learning to pick up the blitz and changing the play accordingly.

I could see how the Lord did not want me to remain inadequate in this area, so He allowed for growth opportunities like this one. I recognized that my attitude needed to be adjusted. I realized that I am capable of handling these situations with a lot more grace. This understanding brought peace to my spirit.

We finally got into the car and headed to church. I spent the entire drive apologizing to Tiffani and Carol. I expressed my disappointment in how I reacted to them. I told them that I hated the conflict and that this was something I was going to learn to deal with more effectively. I tried to repair the hurt of rejection and shame my comments may have inflicted on them. I reassured them of my love and acceptance. After that, the morning went much better.

We get countless snaps in the game of life. Making good decisions by reading the defense and changing the play, builds unity that can bind us together for a lifetime. These lessons will be the stories that we can pass down from generation to generation. *"You yourselves are our letter, written on our hearts, known and read by everybody. You show that you are a letter from Christ, the result of our ministry, written not with ink but with the Spirit of the living God not on tablets of stone but on tablets of human hearts."* 2 Corinthians 3:2-3

Prayer

Dear Father, we commit ourselves to unity and cooperation. Guide us as we direct our family. Create peace in our hearts, patience in our words, kindness in our attitudes and grace in our thoughts. Amen

CHAPTER 12
ADVERSITY

The trials of my senior season began during a spring game in late April 1985. I had performed pretty well during our practices. I worked hard in the weight room during winter conditioning. I had put on a few pounds and I was bigger, stronger and faster than the previous year. I was the only returning letterman at the quarterback position. My "walk on makes good" dream was in full swing and I was really starting to believe in myself. I was having a solid spring game when I rolled to my right on a run pass option. I decided I could get up field and get a first down so I tucked the ball and started to run. The strong safety came up to make a play and instead of running him over, which was the norm for me, I tried to put a move on him. I planted my right foot and I heard a snap. I collapsed.

I had been down this road before. I had torn the ACL (anterior cruciate ligament) in my right leg the spring of my sophomore year. The rehabilitation for that injury includes at least eight months of grueling, painful exercises. It seemed that all I had worked for was now in limbo. Repairing the ACL would mean the end of my senior year. I spent the remainder of the game signing autographs and lamenting my future.

Surgery was a couple of days later. When it was over I was told that the ACL was torn along with the meniscus. Because I was the only quarterback with any real experience, we decided not to fix the torn ligament. We chose to do rigorous strengthening, taping and fitting a special brace to secure the leg. This seemed like a viable plan. I was grateful not to be in a cast again.

Things deteriorated during the summer rehab. While I was doing a set of squats (a leg strengthening exercise), I felt my back shift. We would later discover that I had a herniated disc. This was extremely discouraging and set me back even more. I had a hard time just lifting weight, so rehab became increasingly difficult. I pressed on and did what I could, knowing that I was now very limited physically.

Carol and I got married August 3, 1985, about two weeks before fall camp started. My father let us use one of his cab-over campers for our honeymoon. (Doesn't everyone go camping after they get married?) My back hurt so badly that I could barely drive. I had to lay flat for an hour after driving just to help relieve the pain. I was miserable. My knee wasn't right, and my back was killing me.

Then the really painful part happened. When we returned from our honeymoon I reported to three-a-day workouts. At the first team meeting we were told that senior walk-on tight end Brian Heimer had committed suicide at his home in Shelby, Nebraska. He was a small town hero. I had just seen him at our wedding. This was devastating to me personally. I served as a pallbearer at his funeral a couple of days later.

I had a torn up knee and a messed up back, I got married, a teammate committed suicide and now practice started. I was not in a very positive frame of mind. I remember going to Coach Osborne's office to air my feelings. I ended up in tears trying to make sense of Brian's death. I was in despair. Coach tried to comfort me. I was having trouble reconciling the trauma I was going through.

Practice started and I was nowhere close to full speed. I had no confidence in planting my right leg. What once was one of my athletic strengths, running, was now a liability. I was slow, unsure and lacked trust in my abilities. It got worse for me when they put a green jersey on me so I wouldn't be hit in practice. I had never seen anyone wear a green jersey before. This was embarrassing. An additional blow came when they chose team captains and I was not elected. I wouldn't have voted for me either. I was a mess and we were opening on national television at home against an improving Florida State football program. I could only hope that somehow when the game started I would perform better than I did in practice. That did not happen. Coach would tell us we only play as well as we practice. As usual, he was right.

If you have ever wondered whether the players on the sidelines hear people in the crowd when they scream at them, the answer is yes. Players may not always hear exactly what the crowd is saying, but they can hear you. Mostly, however, they are trying not to. I played poorly in the first quarter. I called a stupid, unnecessary timeout. I missed open receivers and I was totally ineffective. Coach replaced me with sophomore McCathorn Clayton.

Mac promptly ran sixty yards on an option play, something I couldn't do. Watching him run down the field, I thought my senior season was over. I tried to keep my head up and my mind in the game. We still struggled to put points on the scoreboard. We were down 17-13 at halftime. I started the second half and things didn't get much better, so Mac came in again.

About midway through the fourth quarter Coach Osborne put me back in the game. I could hear the fans booing me vehemently. It was really loud. I love Nebraska fans. They are passionate about their team, they are well-informed and they respect the game. Their expectations are high, and they should be. It still hurts today, however, as I reflect on how it felt to be treated that way by our fans. It was so bad that my mom left the game at half time because she couldn't listen to the fans berate her son. My wife was also in the crowd with my parents. Many around them were so belligerent that my mild-mannered wife finally asked them, "do you think you could do better?" My family was hurting as well. To this day my wife's joy of the Nebraska football experience has been tarnished because of the behavior of a few fans.

The crazy thing was I had the ball late in the game with an opportunity to score and win the game. After all we had been through, we still had a chance. I didn't get it done.

On fourth down I was trying to hit the tight end coming underneath the linebackers. The ball didn't clear our center's helmet. It bounced off his head. Game over. Florida State 17, Nebraska 13. As of 2014, this is still the last home opener that Nebraska has lost.

McCathorn won the starting job for the next game. I was on the bench. I was humiliated by my performance, my confidence was shot and we still had a long season ahead of us. It got so bad for me that I wrote "Phil 4:13" on tape around my wrist just to get me through practice.

The Play: Playing with Pain
"I can do everything through him who gives me strength."
Philippians 4:13

This scripture was my source of commitment and resilience throughout the season. The painful experiences of life often become our most effective teachers. Even though we suffer through these valleys on our journey, the value of these circumstances can exceed the pain. The choice to allow His strength to empower us is ours.

In my life, there are two categories of pain: physical and relational. They both can be debilitating. They both can train us in godliness.

Physical Pain

I have more scars on my body than I care to admit. It's not a good sign when your surgeon is in your smart phone's top ten. I say that not to brag but to let you know that I am well acquainted with discomfort, agitation and considerable amounts of pain. I laugh at the notion of "pain tolerance" as though it is something that is truly measurable. There is no way to quantify another person's suffering, or their ability to manage the discomfort. With athletes this is even more difficult because everyone is trying to hide their pain, or hide behind it. It is hard to tell the difference.

One of the challenges of chronic pain management is knowing what is "normal." If normal is uncomfortable and irritating, you don't know any different and you learn to deal with it. Dealing with it, unfortunately, may lead to other issues like alcoholism, drug use or other forms of self-medication that become even greater obstacles to overcome.

I really did not understand how much pain I was living in until I had a total knee replacement in 2011. For more than twenty-five years I had managed my suffering through gritting my teeth, taking Advil and experiencing anguish. Once I began to heal from the surgery, I had no pain. *No pain!* It was weird. I felt free for the first time in a quarter century. I said to Carol, "No wonder I was so irritable." I did not know how bad I really felt until there was relief.

How we treat our physical pain can dictate our disposition toward our family. We live in a "suck it up" type of manly world that is not conducive to family unity. When in pain I lacked grace and patience. I had to learn to be honest with humility. It was up to me not to allow my discomfort to become an offense to those I love. I have discovered that many men are struggling with the same maladies that I did, and still do.

Relational Pain

Nothing is more painful than dealing with the hurt associated with relationships. It hurts when we feel that we are failing our families. It hurts when we inflict pain on others. It hurts when we get into fights and we can't seem to resolve them. The pain builds up to the point that we don't like being around one another.

How we manage this pain is a determining factor in our success. Do we let the pain keep us from engaging (we stay on the bench) or do we still step onto the field? Do we let the pain of turnovers cripple us? Or do we find the value in all of our aches and pains and stay in the game? If we do, victory is guaranteed. When we are under adversity, we have two choices: Focus or fold.

Obedience

Family life can be a series of painful experiences designed to build our capacity to lead. Jesus himself was a product of pain. *"Although he was a son, he learned obedience from what he suffered and, once made perfect, he became the source of eternal salvation for all who obey him."* Hebrews 5:8-9. Suffering is not something many of us wanted to sign up for, yet that is exactly what we must play through.

As we learn to endure trials we gain valuable insight into ourselves. We discover our absolute need for a savior. This allows us to let our weakness be our strength as we rely upon Him for perspective and insight. We are given the opportunity to be a source of inspiration to those who are watching. Staying with the game plan despite setbacks creates confidence and a willingness to follow in the same way that a general leads the charge into battle regardless of the odds.

Hope

When we are experiencing battle while feeling pain, disappointment and grief, our first task as family quarterback is to keep hope alive. When everything around us is falling apart, our family is looking to us to find a way through the turmoil. Hope is a powerful element.

In his book *Think on these Things*, John Maxwell observed:
- "Hope shines brightest when the hour is darkest.
- Hope motivates when discouragement comes.
- Hope energizes when the body is tired.
- Hope sweetens when the bitterness bites.
- Hope sings when all melodies are gone.
- Hope believes when the evidence is limited.
- Hope listens for answers when no one is talking.
- Hope climbs over obstacles when no one is helping.
- Hope endures hardship when no one is caring.
- Hope smiles confidently when no one is laughing.
- Hope reaches for answers when no one is asking.
- Hope presses toward victory when no one is encouraging.
- Hope brings the victory when no one is winning."

As I struggled with hope in my own life, I discovered that my hope was misplaced. I have a tendency to hope in myself. I placed my hope in my strength, my creativity, my endurance, my passion and my own hard work. When I would let myself down, I let everyone else down as well. This was painful because my hope would dissipate and we all would be left stranded.

Our hope needs to be squarely placed on our relationship to Christ. *"Be strong and take heart, all you who hope in the Lord."* Psalm 31:24

We Need Each Other

Perhaps the most underestimated asset in dealing with pain is fellowship. The Lord wants us to rely on each other for strength when we have none. He desires that we turn to one another for endurance and relief.

My favorite biblical story describing this principle is found in Exodus: 17. The Israelites were going into battle against the Amalekites. Moses went up on a hill to watch. When he held his arms up, the Israelites won. When he tired and dropped his arms, the Amalekites won. It took Aaron and Hur holding up Moses's arms for Israel to win the victory.

We need Aarons and Hurs in our lives to hold us up when we are suffering. During my senior season, I often turned to offensive guard Stan Parker to "hold up my arms." He would encourage me, pray for me and help me get through practice when I couldn't do it on my own.

Our pain has value. It is up to us to find the value. *"In bringing many sons to glory, it was fitting that God, for whom and through whom everything exists, should make the author of their salvation perfect through suffering."* Hebrews 2:10

Reading the Defense
"Humble yourselves before the Lord, and he will lift you up."
James 4:10

For a player there is no more gratifying feeling after a game than to be sore from head to toe. If I wasn't in pain I didn't think I had played hard enough. It was almost a badge of courage to be in total discomfort. This is where I discovered pain meds. I could consume 800 mg tablets of Motrin like they were M&M's. We were given boxes of those precious orange goodies. This was my introduction into medicating.

Managing pain can turn into an art form. Whether it is physical or relational, pain has to be dealt with. The devil wants us to control the side effects of life's irritation in the unhealthiest ways possible. He is going to try to trick us. He loves to use deception and counterfeits to mislead us.

Medicating
I recently had dinner with a former teammate. His body is a wreck. Years of football took its toll on him. When I met him he was at a bar having a stiff drink. When I saw how difficult it was for him to walk, I felt so bad for him. In an effort for him to minimize his pain he uses alcohol as the solution. I couldn't blame him at all. Alcohol is a great pain reliever. I have experienced its sedative effect and it scared me. It would be easy and convenient to medicate in this way.

In the same way there are literally dozens of vices we can indulge in to relieve our pain. This is the devil's grand plan. If he can get us to find freedom from our pain using vices, we won't turn to the true healer. I previously gave a list of some of the activities that we use to isolate ourselves. These also turn into our pain pacifiers. If we allow these vices to control our lifestyle, the enemy wins by keeping us from addressing the real issues.

The most insidious of these devices is pornography. The use of immoral material is an immoral medication for relationship adversity. I have battled this solution in my own life. Self-gratification only leads to greater disconnection and further pain. There is no satisfaction in it. It is the perfect device for the devil to divide and conquer relationships.

The most effective way the enemy keeps us locked down during our suffering is darkness. If he can keep us from identifying our pain, we will never be able to get authentic relief. As I stated earlier, I was not aware of how uncomfortable I was until my pain was gone.

Self-inflicted Pain

Much of what we suffer both physically and relationally is at our own hands. On many occasions while working around the yard Carol could tell that I was hurting and she would encourage me to take break. Out of fear of looking weak I would press ahead. I would finish mowing the lawn, trimming the trees or doing whatever needed to be done. I refused to stop.

The price I paid would be several hours laid out on the bed in severe pain. I would be incapacitated, unable to engage the family, all because I wouldn't listen to my wife. The whole family paid for my pride. Learning to discipline myself, pace my activity and listen to Carol became very beneficial for me.

Relational pain can also be self-inflicted. My family experienced a great deal of sorrow over the years because of my pride, anger and lack of self-control. Proverbs 21:19 is written to help us QB's deal with our family pain. *"Better to live in a desert than with a quarrelsome and ill-tempered wife."*

I have met many women who could be described in the same way. They are all in pain, mostly at the hands of their husbands. There is a saying, "hurting people hurt people." This certainly applied to me. In my pain, I inflicted a great deal of pain on others.

Resentment

There was a toxic mix in the depth of my pain and anger that fueled most of my reactions. That was and is resentment. My resentment and bitterness pointed directly at Carol. She became the focus of all my anxiety, fear and discontent. *"An angry man stirs up dissension, and a hot-tempered one commits many sins."* Proverbs 29:22. That was me. I have also found it to be true for many men. Even the most reserved men are drawn into their own darkness by deep-seated bitterness.

Passive men have a capacity to hide their anger deep in their responses. Usually their anger is only detectable by their wives and children. This can be very deceptive to onlookers. It can appear that this man is very patient, yet he is actually concealing his inner rage. That anger builds over time and eventually spills over to those close to them.

Resentment is like a Trojan horse buried deep in the soul. It is there waiting to wreck havoc. It must be discovered, disarmed and rendered ineffectual. *"Get rid of all bitterness, rage and anger, brawling and slander, along with every form of malice. Be kind and compassionate to one another, forgiving each other, just as in Christ, God forgave you."* Ephesians 4:31-32

Destroy Hope

Like a relentless defense that wants to choke the opponent's will, the devil has his eye set on taking away our future. He wants to demolish our plans and strategies and to destroy our hope. As I stated earlier, hope is a powerful tool for the family quarterback. If the devil can trap us into believing his lies and we succumb to our pain, he can steal our drive, passion and position.

I know too many men who are divorced and have to watch as their former wives remarry. The statistics for children raised in divorced homes repeating this dysfunction are staggering. The confusion caused when children are raised in multiple homes is immense. I am currently working with several couples who have to juggle their children between the various grandparents and step-grandparents. Explaining to a five-year-old why this person is their grandparent and this one is a step-grandparent can be very challenging. Then trying to spell out why their "real" grandma and grandpa are not together makes for very complicated holidays. This is why many couples want to be as far away from family as they can at Thanksgiving. The devil just laughs at this.

The devil does provide some specific responses for you during adversity. If he can get you to make calls from *his* playbook, he can get you to inflict lots of damage. I have subjected my family to every one of these:

- **Retaliate**

  This was my favorite. If I could get angry enough no one could get close to me. I wouldn't have to deal with the pain I was in. I could isolate myself and stay in the darkness. This resulted in me lashing out at Carol or the kids. I inflicted pain in their lives and reproduced the suffering I was experiencing.

- **Retreat**

  Passive men tend to take this route. They blend into the woodwork hoping no one will notice them. If they disappear they can remain blameless in their own eyes. This means someone else has to take the leadership role. A man cannot have his leadership authority taken. He can, however, relinquish it.

- **Reason**

  I could come up with more excuses than you could possibly imagine. If I could deflect responsibility, I would do it every time. This keeps me from facing my sin and the affects it has on everyone.

- **Retire**

  We walk off the field in surrender. When the going gets tough, the devil wants us to give in. If we will quit on this play, we will be more likely to withdraw in the next struggle as well. Resignation can become a lifestyle if we let it.

We love to tell our children that life isn't fair. The only way they can understand this truth is by watching us turn lemons into lemonade. The devil is determined to get you to suck on those lemons instead of drinking the lemonade.

The Red Zone

"Be on your guard; stand firm in the faith; be men of courage; be strong. Do everything in love."
1 Corinthians 16:13-14

Carol and I recently attended a Christian conference in southern California. It was the most refreshing experience we have ever had at a conference. It was as if the speakers checked their egos at the door, filled themselves with grace and distributed that tenderness to the attendees throughout the weekend. When we left I was so inspired that this book was the result of my enthusiasm. I did more writing in the three weeks following that special event than I had in the previous two months.

One of my favorite speakers started his talk by saying, "I have spent over $10,000 in marriage counseling." Rarely are headliners this transparent, especially in Christian settings. He went on to describe a fundamental contradiction. "We applaud when couples get pre-marital counseling. We congratulate them on trying to do it right. If, however, you are getting counseling after the ceremony, we ask, 'What is wrong with you?' It seems ridiculous that we don't honor getting the help we need." I wish I could have taped this speech. It would be the perfect marketing tool for our work.

I met Ken Nair on the set of Trinity Broadcast Network studios in the spring of 1987. I was still coaching in Lincoln. Carol and I were attending an athletes' conference in Phoenix. The conference was hosted by the same organization that would hire me and move us to Arizona. I was at the studio to share what was happening at the conference. Ken was there to promote his book *Discovering the Mind of a Woman.* I let him know that I wasn't too good at this husband thing. He gave me a copy of his book. This started a twenty-five-year relationship.

After we moved to Arizona, Ken began to disciple me weekly. He knew I had an anger problem and he kept trying to get me to deal with it. I resisted. I tried harder to conceal my bitterness but eventually I would blow up again. This was a vicious cycle that led to Carol leaving me.

The hard work began after she came home and we started to reconcile. The process seemed like one step forward and two steps back. My resentment kept sending us in the wrong direction. One day after a major blow up I went into Ken's office and I started venting my resentments, telling him all the things Carol was doing wrong. He stopped me after I had listed about five items. He wrote them down, gave me the list and said, "There is the start to your list. Go work on it." This was the beginning of what I call my resentment defrag. Like a computer needs to have all the junk cleaned out and the hard drive consolidated so it can function properly, I needed to have my spirit cleaned out to remove the toxic waste of resentment.

My anger was debilitating my ability to lead. I was constantly disqualifying myself because of attitude. I could be "right" about a topic and not "righteous" in the way I communicated. I got sick of the terrible cycle we seemed to be stuck in. It was up to me to wrestle with my flesh, get it under control and start enjoying life.

I would go to a local park early in the morning with my Bible, a yellow pad and a pen. I would sit, read, pray and write down my list of resentments. I eventually had pages. This list was never for Carol to see. It was between the Lord and me to hash out. I would go over the list and ask the Lord to show me what he wanted me to learn from each of the items. Some answers came quickly, others more slowly.

For example, one of my hot buttons was our home school classroom. The place was a mess. It was disorganized and embarrassing to look at. It was a source of contention between us. I was frustrated and brought my grievance to the Lord.

"How long has this been an issue?" He asked me.

"A long time," I told him.

"What have you done about it?"

"Nothing," was all I could say.

"Then why are you mad at her? You haven't done anything to help her, or even inquire as to what you could do. You are just mad. What has that gotten you so far?"

He was right! I needed to get involved and find out how I could help. I sat down patiently with Carol and asked her what I could do to assist. She said, "I could really use some book shelves for the school room. The place is a mess and it drives me crazy." She felt the same way I did, and she gave me specific instructions to help. Yes, this actually worked! Instead of being mad, I could lead us to a peaceful place through the help of the Holy Spirit.

The Lord did this same thing with countless other items on my yellow pad. I would do this for many months. Even today if I feel bitterness creeping into my heart I get out a pen and pad. I am not afraid to share these conversations I have with Jesus, because they happen.

That may be the first place you need to start. Talk to Jesus, wait, listen and He will speak to you. We have to eradicate the nasty, bitter attitudes that create disconnection.

It also helps to have other brothers in our lives to challenge us. These "iron sharpens iron" relationships are an imperative part of a family quarterback's life. Did you know Peyton Manning still has a quarterback coach? Yes, he does.

Prayer

Dear Lord, help me see the resentment that keeps me from peace, contentment and patience. Show me the attitudes that separate me from my family. Speak to my heart and lead me in the way everlasting. Amen

Chapter 13
Play Until the Whistle Blows

My first three years at the University of Nebraska I didn't follow Jesus. I had accepted Christ into my life at the age of eight, but I didn't let that mess with me too much. My junior year of high school I had attended a Fellowship of Christian Athletes (FCA) Weekend of Champions where Nebraska Quarterback Tom Sorely was speaking. I went forward to receive Christ again. I thought that perhaps it didn't work the first time.

I remember that I quit cussing, for a week or two. That was the totality of my conversion. I must admit that I have felt the presence of God since I was young, I just didn't allow it to affect me a great deal. My girlfriend at the time gave me a Bible that intrigued me. When that girl was gone, so was my devotion.

After three years of college I was on the brink of obscurity. I was fortunate that they didn't recruit any scholarship quarterbacks in my class. They did give six scholarships to amazing quarterbacks over the next two years. They were all better athletes than I was.

In February of 1984 my life was heading toward the junk yard. I was skipping class, smoking pot and drinking excessively. After a total knee reconstruction and a shoulder surgery, things didn't look good for me on the field or in life. I decided to attend another FCA meeting on campus. At that event legendary Husker player Jeff Kenny gave his testimony of faith. I figured I had nothing to lose so when he asked if there was anyone who wanted to commit their life to Christ, I raised my hand emphatically. I knew I was trying to save my life through football and that wasn't working out very well. Maybe the third time would be a charm. I didn't see visions. Lightning didn't strike. There were no miracles. Yet, something was different. I picked up my Bible again. The presence of God I had always felt was stronger now. I started to pay attention to it. I began to listen.

That spring was pivotal for my career. Our spring practices would last for four long weeks. We scrimmaged twice a week. It was almost a survival of the fittest. I started the workouts as the number two quarterback behind Craig Sundberg. Craig was a senior who had waited his turn to play and was the heir apparent to Turner Gill. I was competing with two sophomores and four talented freshman to be Craig's backup. I was a long shot. A player's place on the depth chart is only good up until the next scrimmage. The players then move up or down according to their performance.

My number two spot was only guaranteed for a couple of days as I entered spring training. I had to earn the right to keep it. I was not the most gifted athlete so I had to make up for it with grit, knowledge, execution and hustle. Something in my soul began to renew my courage and confidence. For my whole life, I had tried to impress people through my abilities. I had found much of my value through football and now that seemed like it was ending. I decided to go out and just have fun. I quit trying so hard and just enjoyed the game.

That first practice the wind was blowing like crazy. When we started throwing long patterns it was hard to get the ball out that far in the breeze. Still, I could make that throw. I realized that I was as capable as any of the other guys. I began believing in myself. I knew the offense. I understood what we were trying to accomplish. My confidence started to soar.

I started running the ball with authority. I really enjoyed the physical contact and it showed. Instead of being apprehensive or cautious, I became a bull. I was bigger than the defensive backs. Since I couldn't outrun them, I decided I would try to run them over. I was able to make a play with determination and drive. The coaches seemed to appreciate my aggressive style.

I kept my second spot all the way through the spring. I had a solid spring game and I even arguably outplayed Craig. They rewarded with me a scholarship. It was then that I knew Jesus had changed my life and freed me to be the quarterback that I was capable of being. With every interview, I gave Him the glory.

The fall of 1984 Craig and I were one and one-A on the depth chart. I would practice with the first team and Coach promised that I would get to play. (I just broke down in tears as I wrote that.) The first two games I played a lot and scored a few times. We were moving up the national rankings and we headed to UCLA for a game as the number one team in the country.

We beat the Bruins and our I-back Jeff Smith made the cover of *Sports Illustrated*. We traveled to Syracuse to play a team we had beaten by 100 or so points the year before. We were living large. Then reality hit. We were ambushed in the Carrier Dome. Craig banged up his shoulder the week prior and wasn't quite right yet. The noise in the dome was deafening. We couldn't get anything going on offense and we lost 17-9.

We started the Big Eight schedule the next week with Oklahoma State. Craig threw a couple of interceptions in the first half and Coach gave me the nod. I played adequately, completed some critical passes including one that went for a touchdown. Shane Swanson returned a punt for a touchdown and we beat the Cowboys 17-3.

The play that got Coach's attention wasn't one that I expected. During film session Coach was methodically going through each play. He kept replaying one routine pitch play over and over again. Then he said, "Look at this guy. Now that's effort."

He was referring to me. After making the pitch to our I-back, I turned around to make a block. That was my job. Nobody was there. The play was still taking place, so I ran around the end. I headed up field as the play continued and dove at the safety's legs and took him down. I didn't think anything of this. I thought it was kind of fun. We were taught always to play until the whistle blew. I am convinced that it was my willingness to give extra effort on plays like that which persuaded Coach to give me my first start the following week.

The Play: Perseverance
"Let us not become weary in doing good, for at the proper time we will reap a harvest if we do not give up."
Galatians 6:9

Almost any long running play that happens during a football game has a critical down-field block associated with it. In our offense it was usually the receivers who made those essential blocks. The willingness to never quit during a play inevitably has positive ramifications.

This principle applies to our home life as well. The word "persevere" implies that we will have to go through intense struggles that will require us to make the choice either to continue or to quit. There is no perseverance without an urge to give in. We make decisions daily to persist in our Christian walk or cave in to the devil, our flesh or the culture. These are not choices of salvation, just options of destination. When we give in, we allow the enemy to get a foothold. These detours can interrupt our growth and most certainly our peace.

"Therefore, since we have been justified through faith, we have peace with God through our Lord Jesus Christ, through whom we have gained access by faith into this grace in which we now stand. And we rejoice in the hope of the glory of God. Not only so, but because we know that suffering produces perseverance; perseverance, character; and character, hope. And hope does not disappoint us, because God has poured out his love into our hearts by the Holy Spirit, whom he has given us." Romans 5:1-5

In the last chapter, we discussed the value of hope. The above scripture gives us the recipe for it:

1. **Start with suffering.** Great! That is not what I wanted to begin with either. We must face the fact that this life has suffering attached to it. We cannot avoid it. We must embrace its value. "Join with me in suffering for the gospel, by the power of God," 2 Timothy 1:8b

2. **When we endure suffering the result is perseverance.** The verse from Romans 5 above says "suffering produces perseverance." The word "produces" implies an active process. This does not happen without action. It is a by-product of the suffering completing its task. "You then, my son be strong in the grace that is in Christ Jesus." 2 Timothy 2:1

3. **Perseverance accomplishes character.** Our experiences create and pattern our character. Like metal is molded and shaped in the heat of a furnace, our integrity is formed in testing and trial. "Do your best to present yourself to God as one approved," 2 Timothy 2:15a

4. **Our character creates hope for those who follow us.** This is our reputation, the reputation of our family and the reputation of Christ. This hope is what our wives and children crave from us. "'For I know the plans I have for you,' declares the Lord, 'plans

to prosper you and not to harm , plans to give you hope and a future.'" Jeremiah 29:11

Teachable

The key to perseverance is learning through the process of suffering. When you allow yourself to get an education during the trials of life, the struggles you experience will have meaning. I have watched men exhibit this kind of attitude in their workplaces. We must take that same willingness into our home. The issue is our attitude.

Seeing the Bigger Picture

Step back from your conflicts and drama for a minute. Take a view of your circumstances from 30,000 feet. Is God surprised by what you are facing? I don't think so. Do you believe that He can give you wisdom and insight to navigate this trial? If you really do believe that, wouldn't you drop to your knees and ask him for it? The issue is perspective.

Calling

"And we know that in all things God works for the good of those who love him, who have been called according to his purpose." Romans 8:28. We Christians love to throw this verse around like a life raft to a drowning victim. For me this verse is a question. Am I called according to His purpose even when I face conflict, disappointment or discouraging circumstances? If I am going to gain wisdom, insight and guidance it is up to me to choose whether or not I am a man of God. The issue is calling.

Lessons from *Rocky*

Do you remember the first time you saw the movie *Rocky*? There is no greater icon in Americana than Rocky Balboa. Why? Because we love to see someone take a beating and get back up. Rocky is just like any one of us. We put ourselves into his story. We want to be able to take the pounding that life dishes out and not give in to it. We want to keep getting off the canvas, to never, ever give up.

The following is from a scene from *Rocky VI*. Rocky is talking to his son. Listen to the wisdom and perspective:

"Let me tell you something you already know. The world ain't all sunshine and rainbows. It's a very mean and nasty place, and I don't care how tough you are, it will beat you to your knees and keep you there permanently if you let it. You, me, or nobody is gonna hit as hard as life. But it ain't about how hard you hit. It's about how hard you can get hit and keep moving forward; how much you can take and keep moving forward. That's how winning is done! Now, if you know what you're worth, then go out and get what you're worth. But you gotta be willing to take the hits, and not pointing fingers saying you ain't where you wanna be because of him, or her, or anybody. Cowards do that and that ain't you. You're better than that! I'm always gonna love you, no matter what. No matter what happens. You're my son and you're my blood. You're the best thing in my life. But until you start believing in yourself, you ain't gonna have a life."

Fan or Follower

It would have done me good to hear that speech a few times when Carol and I would get into arguments. I lost her respect because I would not listen to the Holy Spirit. I tried to fight with her instead of fighting with my flesh. When I would give in to my flesh, her confidence in my love and commitment would come into question. That is where we determine our dedication. Are we a follower of Jesus, or just a fan? Fans are fickle. A follower is devoted, is not easily discouraged, is persistent, is faithful and does not quit.

We are required to stay in the game. No retreat. No surrender. It is darkest before the dawn. We made a vow before God that we would love our wives until death do us part. We must commit ourselves to keeping our promises. *"Therefore we do not lose heart. Though outwardly we are wasting away, yet inwardly we are being renewed day by day. For our light and momentary troubles are achieving for us an eternal glory that far outweighs them all. So we fix our eyes not on what is seen but on what is unseen. For what is seen is temporary, but what is unseen is eternal."* 2 Corinthians 4:16-18

Reading the Defense

"I am afraid that just as Eve was deceived by the serpent's cunning, your minds may somehow be led astray from your sincere and pure devotion to Christ."
1 Corinthians 11:3

Deception

The devil is a master of deception. He disguises his defenses well. He tricks you into thinking a blitz is coming from the right when it's actually coming from the left. I have fallen for his misdirection a thousand times. There have been several days when things were going great. We were enjoying life, having fun together. Then, within minutes, the whole world seemed to be falling apart around me. The next thing I knew I was standing in the rubble of a burned down house. It is so hard to clean up the mess, repair the damage and put it all back together again. It feels hopeless. If that is where we end up, we are right where the devil wants us: ready to quit.

Testing the Soil

The devil's plan is spelled out for us to see in Mark 4:14-20. He uses our flesh and the world to deceive us from receiving our calling. *"The farmer sows the word. Some people are like the seed along the path, where the word is sown. As soon as they hear it, Satan comes and takes away the word that was sown in them. Others, like seed sown on the rocky places, hear the word and at once receive it with joy. But since they have no root, they last only a short time. When trouble or persecution comes because of the word, they quickly fall away. Still others, like seed sown among thorns, hear the word; but the worries of this life, the deceitfulness of wealth and the desires for other things come in and choke the word, making it unfruitful. Others, like seed sown on good soil, hear the word, accept it and produce a crop--thirty, sixty or even a hundred times what was sown."*

Let's breakdown this strategy. This is our scouting report. The word is being sown into your life. What kind of soil you are will determine your effectiveness against the devil's scheme.

- **Steals**

  Satan comes and takes it. He does not want you to receive the word of truth and grace. He is going to try to talk us out of the kindness and mercy Jesus offers us. It is important that we learn to hear the small, still voice of the Holy Spirit. It is also critical that we recognize the voice of our enemy. He too will whisper in our ear to take away the seed that has been planted.

  One evening we were in our weekly small group and Carol started to cry because of my attitudes toward her. The leader stopped and asked everyone to pray for me. I was thinking, "I don't need to take this!" I left the meeting and walked the eight miles home. I was listening to the wrong voices.

- **Early success**
  You receive it with joy. There is no root. It lasts a short time. I am famous for the two-week crusade. I would get excited about something, get started and then flame out. Have you ever been to a seminar or conference that you thought changed your life? You get home and the enthusiasm fades faster than you thought it would? Me too. This showed me how shallow my soil was.

- **Challenges**
  Trouble or persecution comes. They quickly fall away. Carol would want to sit down and resolve a past conflict. I would engage her with determination. She would express how much I had discouraged, defeated and hurt her. I couldn't take her reflection of my leadership. I would blow up and create more damage. This revealed my insecurities.

- **Trust**
  Worries about life and money choke the word. Many of our disputes were regarding finances. My identity would be wrapped up in my work and our belongings. I was driven to be successful. I wanted to conquer the world, make money, drive nice cars and look good. When things got tight I would get angry because I couldn't have everything I thought I deserved. When Carol challenged me on my attitude, I reacted badly toward her. This revealed my lack of faith.

The devil fears that we will be like the seed sown on good soil. That soil reaps a crop that will be a threat to the kingdom of darkness. He has to do everything possible to keep that from happening.

Shame

I have mentioned shame several times throughout this book. I see shame as the greatest threat to our reaping a healthy harvest. The devil shows us our sin to cripple us, if we let him. He uses it repeatedly in my life. He throws my turnovers in my face almost daily. *"My disgrace is before me all day long, and my face is covered with shame."* Psalms 44:15

Shame creates isolation, guilt, discouragement and depression. We get depressed when we don't see a way through our struggles. We can't see the path because it must be found on our knees with contrition. Jesus is the answer to our shame. He is the only way out of the prison shame creates.

King David was a man well acquainted with shame. His offenses could have been his undoing. Instead, he chose to seek forgiveness and cleansing. *"Have mercy on me, O God, according to your unfailing love; according to your great compassion blot out my transgressions. Wash away all my iniquity and cleanse me from my sin. Create in me a pure heart, O God, and renew a steadfast spirit within me. Do not cast me from your presence or take your Holy Spirit from me. Restore to me the joy of your salvation and grant me a willing spirit, to sustain me. The sacrifices of God are a broken spirit; a broken and contrite heart, O God, you will not despise."* Psalm 51: 1-2, 10-12, 17

Over the past twenty-five years I have watched too many men quit on their wives, children, friends, family and most importantly Jesus. The culture of divorce in America has to stop. It can only stop when those who want to quit refuse to quit. If men do not allow themselves to be deceived by the devil and if they refuse to give in to his tactics, their shame will pass. Those who choose to reject the voice of their selfish ambition and who choose to resist the devil must choose to follow Jesus.

The Red Zone
"This is the one I esteem: he who is humble and contrite in spirit,
and trembles at my word."
Isaiah 66:2b

I remember the night I learned that I was a quitter. It is like it was yesterday. The memory is so vivid that I can still actually smell the sweat pouring down my face when I realized the truth. It was a fall evening. The air was crisp and cool. It was the kind of night that would be perfect for spending time wrapped in a blanket, sitting under the stars enjoying a warm fire.

That night, however, the only fire our family was experiencing was the blaze of my anger. Carol and I were in the middle of one of our terribly childish interactions. I don't even remember how it started, and it doesn't matter. Our disagreement turned into another hostile exchange that was getting out of control. My typical response to these exchanges was to "out mad" her and hope she would back off. Well, this time she wasn't giving in and I was getting tired of listening to whatever rationale she was using.

So, I grabbed my basketball and headed to the local park. That was a habit I had developed over the previous year or so to blow off some steam and to get some exercise. I got to the park and there were a group of guys playing ball. My attitude was heated and I couldn't wait to get into some good competition. Even though I was still under thirty, my body felt like I was sixty. My knee and back hurt, but I didn't care. Nothing could keep me from playing. I was driven and committed.

After a couple of vigorous games my leg started to swell. My back was getting stiff and I was wondering if I had broken a finger. These were mere inconveniences to an athlete like me because "I always press through. I never quit!" My team lost so we had to sit out and wait to play the winners in the next game.

That's when it happened. You know those moments that transcend time. Everything slows down and it's like you are watching yourself go through an experience in slow motion. As I was sitting on a bench with sweat pouring down my face and pain rushing through my body, the Holy Spirit said to my spirit, "You are such a quitter!"

I couldn't believe what I had just heard. I knew exactly who was talking to me and I was willing to have a discussion. So I said back, "What are you crazy? You know I'm no quitter!" I got no response, just silence. I was guessing maybe He didn't hear me. Or maybe He needed an illustration of who He was talking to. I said, "I'm the guy who played with a torn ACL my entire senior season. I can barely walk right now and you couldn't drag me off this basketball court. I'm no quitter!"

There was an awkward silence. At this point I was a little nervous that the guys around me might think I was some sort of psycho. This conversation was taking place in my heart and mind but at the time it seemed as though it was happening in stereo all around me.

Then the Spirit said to me, "You quit in the only place in life that matters: Home. You quit on Carol. In fact, you always quit on her. I could care less what you do on the football field or basketball court. What I care about is the game of life and in that regard you are a quitter! Whenever it gets tough, when you need to dig down and persevere in your life with Carol, you quit on her. You run out the door and escape."

With tears running down my face I grabbed my ball and headed to the car. I knew I needed to head home. I *really was* a quitter. I had very little willingness to battle through our conflicts. I would either blow up or retreat when I needed to press forward. It embarrassed me to realize my inadequacy. It also inspired me to be more determined, careful and patient. I never wanted to quit on her again.

Prayer

Dear Lord, we must persevere. Strengthen us Lord to have the courage to stay in the battles we face daily. Give us stamina when we are weak. Grant us patience to stay engaged. We need you Lord, to give us the strength not to quit. Amen

Chapter 14
Check with Coach

I spent the entire week heading into the Oklahoma game my junior year giving God praise... for everything. I was bombarded with requests to share my story. I used every interview, every speech, every opportunity to give the glory to the One who deserved it, Jesus Christ.

I was the starting quarterback for the number one team in the country! This was not by accident and I was not going to let it pass without making the most of it. It seemed surreal for me to be getting calls from across the country, posing for pictures, addressing the media, all while the biggest game of my life was just a few days away. This was a once-in-a-lifetime occasion and I was squeezing it. On top of that, I caught a cold so I was feeling lousy.

Everyone in Lincoln looked forward to this week. The hated Sooners were coming to town for the last regular season game. Win this game and we would head to the Orange Bowl to play for a ring (the prize that accompanies the national championship). The place was buzzing and everywhere you went people were talking about that illusive title. It had been twelve years since the Huskers last ended the season as the mythical champion.

The previous season the 1983 team was perhaps the finest group of athletes Nebraska had ever had, yet they came up two points short of a title. Now, in 1984, without the celebrated triplets— Mike Rozier, Turner Gill and Irving Fryer— or Outland Trophy winner Dean Steinkuhler, this team was just two wins from an ultimate glory that no one had predicted. This team was being led by a walk on, no name, small town kid... me.

It was my week to shine, pose for a magazine cover, meet and greet everyone with a smile and proclaim the good news of the gospel. I did all that without flinching. I had a great week of practice despite feeling poorly. I was ready for this game. I had approached it just as I had every game so far that season. We were riding a twenty-seven game conference win streak with twenty-one straight wins at home. It was up to me to do my job. I needed

171

to take care of the ball and wear out the Oklahoma defense so that by the fourth quarter we would be the best team. Then, we could head to Miami for the ultimate prize.

Life, like a football, can take some crazy bounces. I failed to make this fairy tale story end with a celebration. I didn't even get on the field for the fourth quarter.

A fumbled snap on the first series of the game put us behind. Another fumble late in the first quarter made things even worse. I made a bad audible and threw an interception before half time. That sent me to the bench. My dear friend Craig Sundberg came in and played well enough to keep us in the game. A late fumble and a goal line stand kept us from a trip to Florida for the Orange bowl. We eventually lost 17-7, but the game was much closer than that.

As you can imagine, I was devastated after the game. To this day I would say it was one of the most painful, and yet, glorious moments of my life. It was glorious because the Spirit of God met me at the lowest point in my life. When I had failed so badly, He met me there, spoke to my spirit and comforted me.

A staircase connected the player's locker room to the lounge upstairs where the press did the post-game interviews with the players and coaches. I knew I had to face the reporters, their questions and the TV cameras after the game. As I took off my jersey to head upstairs I could feel the pain, disappointment and embarrassment well up in my heart. I was on the verge of breaking down, crying and humiliating myself right there at my locker. So I bolted for the door to the staircase and I sat there on the stairs and began to weep. I can still feel this moment as if it is happening right now.

I was sad, ashamed, rejected, confused, let down and mostly angry. I was upset because I had given God all the praise and glory all week and all season long. I did everything in my power to pass the praise to Him. I had used the platform He had given me to speak to people and I was relentless about it. Yet in my hour of need, in my greatest trial, in the most important football game of my life, it felt like He abandoned me. I fumbled twice and threw an interception. Where was He when I needed Him? *Nowhere!* He left me out in the cold. I had to ask Him about this.

Through my tears I cried out to the Creator, "What did I do wrong? Why are you punishing me? Didn't I praise you all year long? Didn't I testify to your goodness? Didn't I give you glory every time I could?" To my surprise He answered me.

Now, the Lord doesn't talk to me audibly, just in that small, still (sometimes it's louder than other times) voice that I know is His. He said to me, "You are looking at the wrong scoreboard. I don't care about football games. I look at the heart. Your heart. Yes, you did everything I asked of you. You did well. Can that be enough? Will you still give me praise and glory when things don't go your way? How you handle this adversity is what matters to me."

This new perspective gave solace to my soul. I could feel myself relax and the joy of my salvation return. I wiped my tears and headed upstairs to face the media. The sting of losing that game still affects me today. I do, however, have a better grasp on God's view of the scoreboard.

That encounter changed my life. It strengthened, inspired, comforted and empowered me to move forward with total assurance that He was with me. Turnovers happen. We make mistakes. We can cause hurt in other people's lives. We can do damage. Yet His grace can guide us and direct us to overcome anything that we do or don't do. He is not looking for perfection. He knows only Jesus was perfect. He is looking for a heart that is willing, teachable and obedient to His word and His promptings.

Our coach is Jesus. I am learning to check with Him. He is our comfort. He is our strength. He will provide. He is patient. He is kind. He will guide and direct us. He is our savior, if we will let Him be. "*The Lord is my strength and my shield; my heart trusts in him and I am helped.*" Psalm 28:7

The Play: Pray with Purpose
"If my people, who are called by my name, will humble themselves and pray and seek my face"
2 Chronicles 7:14a

It is imperative that the family quarterback commit to consistent, specific and fervent prayer. A willingness to spend time with our wives in humble intercession is critical. I have also found it to be a rare commodity.

Few of the couples we have worked with over the years have expressed a regular connected prayer life.

I am not a "two hours in the prayer closet" kind of guy. I couldn't sit still that long if my life depended on it. I have discovered that conversations with the Coach can happen all the time. I don't have to seclude myself to hear His voice. I am learning to speak plainly to my Maker, and He will speak plainly to me. I will tell you that my prayer life changed when I started working on my resentments.

I have shared this experience with others and some people get a little offended by my bluntness with God. My life changed when I yelled at God. I was irreverent, disrespectful and contentious. I discovered that He could handle my hostilities. He was not offended and He actually greeted my intensity with gladness. I was so frustrated with my life and angry at everything around me that I told Him so. It was as if He said to me, "Well I'm glad you finally decided to have a conversation with me."

It was during this time that He shared insight into my bitterness with me. He honored my hostility with firm tenderness, like He did that night on the basketball court. He was and is direct and caring. He wanted to engage me, just like He wants to engage every man.

Motive

I still lament the decisions I made on the field that day against Oklahoma. I even lay awake at night and wish I had done things differently. I wanted to lead the Huskers to Miami. I could see my picture on the cover of Sports Illustrated. I wanted to get that coveted ring. God's test for me was to see if I was still willing to praise Him even though my dream didn't happen.

The intentions of our prayers will often dictate the results. Let's examine the instructions of Jesus regarding prayer. *"Ask and it will be given to you; seek and you will find; knock and the door will be opened to you. For everyone who asks receives, he who seeks finds; and to him who knocks, the door will be opened. Which of you, if his son asks for break, will give him a stone? Or if he asks for a fish, will give him a snake? If you then, though you are evil, know how to give good gifts to your children, how much more will your Father in heaven give good gifts to those who ask him!"* Matthew 7:7-11

I find it fascinating that Jesus used parenting as a guide for us. So let's consider this:

If your child wanted a brand new car, would you give it to her? I don't think so. You may help guide her into understanding the value of such things but you probably wouldn't just give it to her. She wouldn't appreciate it. Would a new car be a good gift? I think not. Yet, we often pray for such things. We pray for stuff rather than for understanding.

If your child wanted to get straight A's in school, would you negotiate with his teacher for this? Of course not. You would guide your child to discover the needed study habits to achieve this goal. We often pray for an easy road with fewer obstacles and with fewer difficulties. This too would not be a good gift.

What motivates us to pray? Do we desire wisdom, insight and purpose? If we want to know Him better He will grant our wishes.

Contentment

Jesus wants to have a relationship with us. At the heart of any deep fellowship is time spent together. Conversation is what creates intimacy. He wants us to experience His peace. The only way we can is to ask for it. He loves to engage us, but it will be on our terms. He wants us to *want* to be with Him. He will not force Himself on us.

If we are serious about engaging the creator, Psalm 139:23-24 is a great place to start. I call this the guaranteed prayer. He will answer you, but you had better buckle up for it. *"Search me, O God, and know my heart; test me and know my anxious thoughts. See if there is any offensive way in me, and lead me in the way everlasting."* Sin is what separates us from Him. Our disobedience hinders our connection. This verse can lead us to a rapport with God that can last a lifetime.

- *Search me, know my heart*
  Are we open to God searching through our lives and our browser history? If we want to commune with Him we have to want Him in our private places—not to condemn us, but to assist us and to free us from the chains of sin. He wants to cleanse us from the filth of this world. He can only do that with our permission. If we fear His rejection, we cannot enjoy his kindness and grace.

- ***Test me***

  Like a coach who puts you into the varsity game to see how you will do, God wants to put us in situations that will stretch us. Are we willing to get in the game to discover our strengths and weaknesses? The only way we find those things out is through the tests and trials of life. If we ask Him to test us, He will. We often see those tests as punishment rather than as compliments from God. He will not test us past our ability. *"God is faithful; he will not let you be tempted beyond what you can bear."* 1 Corinthians 10:13b. He wants to prepare you for everything.

- ***Know my anxious thoughts***

  Of course, He already knows you are anxious. He wants you to know it. Self-awareness is a key ingredient to advancing in maturity. *"Come to me, all you who are weary and burdened, and I will give you rest."* Matthew 11:28. This includes our anger, frustration and pain. He wants to enter into our suffering and comfort us. He can't help us if we are not honest with ourselves and with Him.

- ***See if there is any offensive way***

  This is a dangerous prayer. Your wife talking with you about an angry exchange you had earlier just might be your prayer's answer. She may let you know how your attitude is disappointing and discouraging to her. You had better have the belt of truth strapped on. *"My son, do not despise the Lord's discipline and do not resent his rebuke, because the Lord disciplines those he loves, as a father the son he delights in."* Proverbs 3:11-12

- ***Lead me in the way everlasting***

  He will guide us if we let Him. We must have an ear to hear His instructions and a heart open to changing direction. We will need help finding the *"narrow road that leads to life, and only a few find it."* Matthew 7:14b. It is worth our time and energy to receive His assistance as we make game plans and strategies. He wants to see us enjoy the victories that are in store for those who love Him.

"Our Father in heaven, hallowed be your name, your kingdom come, your will be done on earth as it is in heaven. Give us today our daily bread. Forgive us

our debts, as we also have forgiven our debtors. And lead us not into temptation, but deliver us from the evil one." Matthew 6:9-13

Reading the Defense:
"Fight the good fight, holding on to faith and a good conscience. Some have rejected these and so have ship wrecked their faith."
1 Timothy 1:18b-19

If the devil can keep us from communicating with the Coach, he disables our offense. Then the family quarterback can only run the offense from a deficient perspective. This is dangerous for the overall game plan. When left to him, the family quarterback will be limited, inhibited and ineffective. *"For my thoughts* (game plan*) are not your thoughts, neither are your ways* (plays*) my ways," declares the Lord. As the heavens are higher than the earth, so are my ways higher than your ways and my thoughts than your thoughts."* Isaiah 55:8-9

Satan wants to cut off the contact between the Father God and His quarterbacks. He wants to eliminate any play calling that comes from heaven. Volumes could be written about man's struggle with prayer. There are hundreds of reasons we don't engage with the creator. I would like to examine three significant factors that limit a man's humble engagement with Father God.

Impatience

We live in a world of instant gratification. That includes fast money, fast food, fast phones, fast cars, fast relationships, fast Internet and fast results. This leads to impatience. We don't naturally wait for anything. We don't even wait for our kids to be born. We induce.

The world revolves around our convenience. If we have to wait in line too long, we leave. If the browser doesn't load quickly, we yell at our laptop. If the person driving in front of us is taking their time, we honk the horn.

We jam so many activities into our day we don't have time to breath. We hurry from event to event without enjoying the ride. Rushing in traffic, texting while driving, running yellow lights, we arrive at our destinations frustrated, angry and exhausted.

When we do take time to pray, it is more like ordering at In-N-Out Burger than engaging the King of Kings. Can I have this, that and the other thing? Oh yes, I do want fries with that! We wait for a moment, nothing happens. We want answers now. We don't have time to wait.

We must consider a contrast. What if you could get tickets to your favorite sporting event, say The Super Bowl or the Masters golf tournament? How long would you wait in line for those tickets? Yes, me too. The things we really want are worth our time. I have seen men take weeks, months, even years to rebuild cars that they loved. Some guys can get up before dawn, brave the cold weather and sit in a tree stand for hours waiting for that prized buck. Or they might wade into cold water, casting their line over and over again just to hook a fish; a fish that they then throw right back into the water. Have you seen a man take his time lining up a putt as if his life depended on it? This too is meaningless.

Ask a man to spend thirty minutes of quiet reflection with Jesus every day and he loses his mind. Ask that man to hold his wife's hand and pray with urgency on a consistent basis, and he may want to beat you up. Something is wrong with the fabric of our faith when we refuse to pray passionately with our family.

Unbelief

Do we really believe the God of the universe hears us? If we did, wouldn't we talk to Him all the time? Of course we would. Our devotion to prayer is a direct reflection of our faith. The enemy does everything in his power to keep us from believing. He attacks our faith on a daily basis.

Even the most faithful men struggle with belief. One of my favorite Bible stories is found in 1 Kings Chapter 18. Elijah the prophet of God faces down the prophets of Baal. In a showdown in front of the whole kingdom, Elijah had the faith to call down fire from heaven to burn up a sacrifice. That had to take some serious trust. The fascinating part of this story is what happens in the next Chapter. Jezebel the wife of Ahab threatened Elijah with his life. *"Elijah was afraid and ran for his life."* 1 Kings 19:3a. He then prayed, *"I have had enough, Lord, Take my life; I am no better than my ancestors."* 1 Kings 19:4b. What? One minute he has so much faith that he brings fire from heaven, then the next minute he is running from a woman asking God to kill him?

I certainly can relate to Elijah. There are some days I feel like I can conquer the world. Then the next day I'm lying in bed feeling worthless. The enemy knows how fragile our faith can be. He wants to twist us into believing God won't show up.

Let us consider Simon Peter, The Rock. He was an assertive follower of Jesus. He was the middle linebacker who took a sword to one of the men arresting Jesus. Yet Jesus said, *"Simon, Simon, Satan has asked to sift you as wheat. But I have prayed for you, Simon that your faith may not fail. And when you have turned back, strengthen your brothers."* Luke 22:31-32. If Peter was going to be sifted to have his faith and trust revealed, don't you think you are worth as much as Peter? You are. Jesus knew that Peter needed to be humbled. Peter needed to see his failing faith. Jesus also wanted him to *"turn back, strengthen your brothers."* We have the same calling. Family quarterbacks, turn back. Strengthen your family.

Shame

I have touched on this topic several times. It is the devil's principle tool to keep us from engaging one another and most importantly the Lord of Lords. *"I see another law at work in the members of my body, waging war against the law of my mind and making me a prisoner of the law of sin at work within my members."* Romans 7:23. This law is the law of sin and its condemnation of man. Sin entraps us in darkness. The good news is found in Romans 7:24-25. *"What a wretched man I am! Who will rescue me from this body of death? Thanks be to God--through Jesus Christ our Lord!"* The devil wants to keep me from the only one who has the keys to the prison cell: Jesus.

The Red Zone
"Seek first his kingdom and his righteousness,"
Matthew 6:33a

Carol and I have had the privilege of telling our story in seminars and classes across the country. In one of our sessions we discuss the issue of prayer within the context of marriage. Praying together had been a major struggle for us. I could pray with everyone, for anything, anywhere and at any time. Praying with Carol was a different story.

It was difficult for her to see me so passionate about caring for others, while in our personal life, I did not readily engage. We discovered that we had a common conflict. One night in our small group we decided to do a little problem solving on this topic. In our discussion we found that men and women were approaching the idea of praying together with totally different emotional considerations. We put these reactions on a white board so we could examine closely what we were experiencing.

When wives suggested prayer, the men were feeling:

- Anxious. What can we do now? She wants to pray. Just as I was getting the upper hand on the argument, she drops Jesus into the conversation.

- Inadequate. Our wives usually are the ones who ask for prayer. We are supposed to be the spiritual leader yet she is suggesting that we turn to Christ, again. We have feelings of failure, guilt and inadequacy. Shame fills our minds.

- Cornered. You know what happens when you corner a big dog? He shows you his fangs. We feel cornered. There is nowhere to run and hide.

- Angry. Our wives want to pray and it makes us mad? That should not be the case. Yet, that is exactly what we may be feeling.

- Embarrassed. We feel like a loser. We get ourselves into these situations then, we can't get us out. We hate it when this happens, especially when it happens over and over again.

- Trapped. There is nothing we can do, but surrender. Why does it feel so terrible to surrender to Jesus?

The amazing contrast in the couples' responses was how the women were impacted when their husbands would offer to pray.

The women felt:

- Hopeful. Maybe we can finally get somewhere. There is a chance that we can reconnect and resolve our differences.

- Encouraged. Now, we can feel close, connected and experience true intimacy.

- Cared for. He really does care about me. He cares about my thoughts and emotions. He wants to lead us to a better place.

- Loved. When we turn to Jesus, she knows we truly love her. We are not going to continue down the same old road that leads to pain.

- Peaceful. She could finally relax because he was going to lead.

The insight we gained from this exchange of views was extremely beneficial.

The family quarterback has to work through his emotional blocks to engage in meaningful prayer with his team. Every man wants his wife to feel loved. To help her feel that way, we need to process our anger and to identify our defensiveness. Our flesh is conspiring against our success. We must subdue its influence, capture its considerations and correct our thinking. *"The weapons we fight with are not weapons of the world. On the contrary, they have divine power to demolish strongholds. We demolish arguments and every pretension that sets itself up against the knowledge of god, and we take captive every thought to make it obedient to Christ."* 1 Corinthians 10: 4-5

Now, it's game time. Prepare for impact. Accept your calling. Read the playbook. Take the snap. Get in the game. Huddle up. Communicate clearly. Lead by example. Take responsibility. Overcome the turnovers. Create unity. Play with pain. Most of all, pray with purpose. Amen!

Prayer

Dear Lord, we love our wives. We want to lead them with courage, enthusiasm and hope. Help us to be the Family Quarterback that you have called us to be. Amen

ACKNOWLEDGMENTS

My 'Hall of Fame' wife Carol—Thanks for showing me what love really looks like.

Tiffani Turner Harding—My amazing daughter, you are a fabulous wife and mother. You will always be my little girl.

Mark Harding—Blessed to have you as a son-in-law. Thanks for being an excellent example of a learner's spirit.

Taylor "Buddy" Turner—My son, whom I am proud of. Your courage and resilient heart will take you far.

Divine Romance Ministry Board:
 Dean and Trudy Volk—Your friendship inspires us daily.
 Len and Tracy Munsil—Your example of faithfulness is priceless.

Divine Romance Ministry Supporters—Thanks for believing in us. This book would not have happened without your generosity.

Mike and Michelle Stillman—Your trust in us gave us courage to follow through on our dreams.

Zach and Lisa Shepherd—Your beautiful family made a great cover picture.

Pastors:
 Mark Buckley—You will always be my pastor. Thank you for over 25 years of friendship. You gave me a job when I needed it. You conducted the wedding of my precious little girl. You loved my parents until they passed. You have always been there for me.

 Travis Hearn—You may recognize a few of your sermons points in this book.

Dave Argue—Thanks for believing in me, for conducting our marriage ceremony, for dedicating Tiffani. I will remember you forever.

Ken Nair—Thank you for helping me arrest my flesh and learn to surrender to Christ.

Eldon Post—Thank you for teaching me to illustrate godliness and humility.

Coach Tom Osborne—I am grateful for the living example of Christ that you are. You have created a legion of men that know what true godly leadership is.

Proofreading friends:
    Luke Carlson
    Mark Fisher
    Jordan Plank

Editors:
    Jon and Kathy Casey—Your help was an amazing gift to us.
    Cindy Conger—It was wonderful to be reunited with you.

The Storyline Conference—Donald Miller and company gave me the inspiration to make this project happen.

Brené Brown—You changed my view of shame, vulnerability and courage.

About the Author

Travis Turner is the founder of Divine Romance Ministries Inc, a ministry dedicated to restoring marriages through inspiration, education and mentoring. Travis has been training men in the area of family relationships for over 20 years. As a former starting quarterback with the University of Nebraska in 1984-85, Travis has experienced both success and failure in ministry, business and family life. He has an adept ability to inspire men to grasp their God-given authority and use it with grace and purpose.

Married in 1985, Travis and his wife Carol, have two adult children and two grandchildren. They share their story of marriage restoration at seminars, retreats and conferences. Travis takes a unique blend of ministry, business and sports experience to inspire leadership in the home, where it belongs.

For relationship resources or to book a speaking engagement, connect with Travis and Carol at:
www.DivineRomanceMinistries.org
www.FamilyQB.org